NEW LEADERSHIP FOR WOMEN AND MEN

Building an Inclusive Organization

NEW LEADERSHIP FOR WOMEN AND MEN

Building an Inclusive Organization

Michael Simmons

Gower

Published by
Gower Publishing Limited
Gower House
Croft Road
Aldershot
Hampshire GU11 3HR
England

Gower
Old Post Road
Brookfield
Vermont 05036
USA

British Library Cataloguing in Publication Data

Simmons, Michael
New leadership for women and men: building an inclusive
organization
1.Leadership
I.Title
658.4'092

ISBN 0 566 07474 5

Library of Congress Cataloging-in-Publication Data

Simmons, Michael.
New leadership for women and men: building an inclusive organization
/ Michael Simmons.
p.   cm.
Includes bibliographical references and index.
ISBN 0–566–07474–5
1. Leadership.   2. Diversity in the workplace.   I. Title.
HD57.7.S54 1996
658.4'092—dc20   96–900
                                                                 CIP

Typeset in Garamond and Avant Garde by Bournemouth Colour Press and printed in Great Britain by Hartnoll's Ltd, Bodmin.

CONTENTS

LIST OF FIGURES

PREFACE

In recent years many books have been written about leadership and its importance in improving the performance of organizations. However, this book is the first to place building an 'inclusive organization' and the elimination of discrimination and prejudice at the centre of its argument and programme for change. In particular, it is the first book to focus on the effects of oppression and gender conditioning on the leadership of women and men.

I believe building successful organizations requires that we put people at the heart of everything we do. This means developing strategies that include everyone within the enterprise in planning and deciding upon the future direction of the business and in contributing to the continual improvement of how the enterprise functions. When people are excluded they feel marginalized, their morale suffers and they are unable to give their best to the organization.

I have used the phrase 'building an inclusive organization' to describe the process of taking positive action to bring everybody into every aspect of the work of the enterprise. It means welcoming people with all their diversity of backgrounds and abilities because they add a value to performance that those who 'fit' the existing profile of people in the organization are unable to offer. They are not 'safe' but they bring excitement and energy and new competencies into the heart of the business.

Applying the concept of 'inclusion' to our organizations is new, but I think it expresses perfectly the next step for those of us who are committed to the goals of involving and empowering everyone in the enterprise. It reaches beyond equality to an organization where no boundaries or limitations are placed on anyone.

The main block to establishing an 'inclusive organization' is the way that discrimination and prejudice operate to exclude members of particular groups. In my experience, discriminatory practices and prejudices towards any individual or group of people, using the excuse of their gender, race, disability, or any other aspect of their identity, is the biggest single reason for the waste of human potential in most enterprises and in society as a whole.

Discrimination and prejudice affect everyone, and work to eliminate them both is crucial to increasing the effectiveness of the organization as a whole as well as improving the working life of every person involved. The key to their elimination is the development of a new leadership committed to releasing the intelligence, creativity and initiative of people at all levels of the organization, particularly those people who have been traditionally excluded from leadership.

Since the beginning of the Industrial Revolution women have faced exclusion and organizations have suffered enormously as a consequence. Strategies to bring women into the centre of the enterprise during the past 15 years have been very successful but much remains to be done. A younger generation of women are knocking at the door and it is time to take a decisive leap and start using the knowledge and skills that women can offer in order to transform the way that things get done. Women at all levels must take up this challenge and settle for nothing less than everything in their pursuit of empowerment.

Men have dominated almost every enterprise in terms of numbers and status, but I believe they have excluded themselves as human beings in some very important ways. They have built organizations into systems that do not value people and in the process do not value men either. The challenge for men is to bring their whole selves into their work and reach beyond that to an era of cooperation and involvement that will optimize the contribution that everyone can make, especially women.

In the United States, as in other countries, there is a growing backlash by some groups of white men against the affirmative action legislation that has helped large numbers of women and black people to begin to take an equal place within, and at senior levels in, our organizations. Therefore, we must move quickly to review our policies and strategies to ensure that men are fully included in everything we do. Any approach that leaves a group of people feeling excluded must need careful scrutiny and change.

BACKGROUND TO THIS BOOK

This book is based on work that was first conceived some 15 years ago. A number of people working in the fields of organization development and equal opportunities came together to explore how to use training more effectively to help organizations to meet the legal requirement that they provide equality of opportunity to those groups of people in society who are known to suffer discrimination.

Legislation had led many managers to review their personnel policies on such matters as recruitment, promotion, pay and other working conditions. However, the contribution that training was able to make to improving the delivery of equal opportunities was still limited and, where it did take place, somewhat limited in its effectiveness. During the past ten years or so, we have worked to develop new perspectives on the issues that underlie inequality of opportunity and have begun to understand the concept of the 'inclusive organization' as one which works systematically to ensure everyone has an opportunity to contribute.

This has led to the development of new thinking about the issues of leadership, new understanding about the role of oppression in determining the opportunity and ability of people to lead, and new understanding of the different issues that women and men face in leading well in these rapidly changing times. As a result, we are developing new strategies and approaches for implementing equal opportunity initiatives, new training designs and new training skills.

This book describes my current understanding, thinking and practice based upon this work.

WHO IS THE BOOK AIMED AT?

It is aimed, first and foremost, at the person in a formal leadership position who feels that she or he is in the middle of a maelstrom, yet is looking for more than a simple or traditional view about what is really going on or what to do about it. It is aimed at anyone who can imagine that it might be possible to relate to these turbulent times as the biggest challenge of their lives, rather like enjoying a giant roller coaster with full commitment and thoroughgoing excitement at every turn. It is aimed at all the people who would like to review their leadership and develop a new approach that is realistic and effective.

It is aimed at those organization and management development specialists who are attempting to reach beyond their traditional understanding to something more radical. It is aimed at equal opportunities specialists who are committed to developing thinking and strategies that will lead to fundamental change in our society and in the common enterprise.

But more than anyone else, it is aimed at all the women and men who have acknowledged that something in the way they have been brought up, something in the expectations that have been placed upon them as young people and in their early working career, and something about the way the organization treats them today because of their gender, is getting in the way of their functioning to their true potential.

THE AIM OF THE BOOK

The central aim of the book is to introduce people to the concept of the 'inclusive organization' and the role of leadership in building it. It examines the role played by institutional discrimination and prejudice in determining the effectiveness of leaders at all levels of organizations and looks in particular at the leadership development needs of women and men.

The intention is to review the situation that we face throughout the world and especially in the developed West. I shall attempt to demonstrate that we are in the grip of a global crisis, that this crisis is fundamentally economic and that the primary response to this crisis during the past 20 years has itself fuelled the crisis and had a huge impact on people's leadership and social relationships at work.

I shall propose that the key challenge in moving us forward is to put people at the heart of everything we do. To do this we need to develop a profound understanding of how valuable each human being is and learn how to involve them fully in every process. Developing a new leadership that works towards understanding the whole situation and decides to see to it that everything in it goes well is crucial to that challenge.

I shall show that there are three goals of transformation and three key activities needed to achieve them. The goals are

- Managing a turbulent environment;
- Increasing productivity and quality;
- Building an 'inclusive organization'.

These goals require us to develop a shared vision and involve everyone in planning how to achieve it, initiate strategies that will lead to continual improvement and innovation, and eliminate discrimination and prejudice.

I plan to show that institutional discrimination and prejudice are the principal causes of the under-use of people's potential in a common enterprise and that both are rooted in a wider system of oppression. My intention is to examine in detail the impact of oppression upon women and upon men as leaders and to propose next steps for each gender if they are to fulfil their potential. I shall introduce the concept of the 'inclusive organization' and offer strategies and experience from my own work as examples of how to move towards such a model.

The book is divided into the following three parts:

- Part I   The Importance of Leadership
- Part II   Developing Women and Men as Leaders
- Part III Building an Inclusive Organization

The contents of each Part is introduced at the beginning of the part.

Writing this book has been an exciting and challenging journey for me. The world in which I live has been in crisis for much of the period of writing, and I have been forced to review where I stand and what I need to do throughout this project; the practice and lessons in this book have been carved out of that experience. I very much hope that readers find this a text that will facilitate making more sense of a world that is in danger of spinning out of control, and help with claiming leadership and how to take complete charge of the situation. As I often say to the people I work with, 'Remember who you really are! If you can remember who you really are there is nothing that you cannot handle and then enjoy!' I wish you well on that journey.

Michael Simmons

ACKNOWLEDGEMENTS

❖

In completing this book, I wish to acknowledge the work of Rosemary Brennan and in particular the unique contribution she has made and the thinking that she has developed in her work with women in organizations. Her work has contributed a great deal to and underpins much of the understanding on which this book is based. However, any failures or limitations in that understanding as expressed in this book are mine and mine alone.

I also deeply appreciate 20 years of learning from the teaching of Harvey Jackins, a man still little known and unrecognized in the wider world for his role in carving out a profound understanding of the inherent nature of human beings and the effects of oppression upon that nature. He taught about and is a model for me of how to put great leadership into practice.

I am deeply indebted to the thinking and leadership of Charlie Kreiner. Charlie has systematically mapped out the nature of the oppression of men and taught large numbers of us throughout the world the importance of loving ourselves and caring deeply for others.

I also appreciate the many colleagues and friends I have found through the years who have worked with me to develop our thinking and practice. In particular Raymond Cadwell, a great Irishman who has supported and loved me as every man should be loved by his best man friend.

Finally I would like to thank the many clients who risked giving me the opportunity to train their people while I continued to learn my trade. I thank you all with great respect and wish you well in your own continuing journeys.

MS

PART I
THE IMPORTANCE
OF LEADERSHIP

❖

Few moments in history have been so pregnant with possibilities. A world-wide crisis in our economic and social system has affected every aspect of our lives and we are challenged as never before to review our approach to working together in a common enterprise. In Part I, I set out an overview of the situation we are in and proposals for the steps we need to take to deal with it effectively.

In Chapter 1, 'Making Sense of The Present', I describe the present situation in the global economy and its impact on our society and lives. I argue that the key challenge is to put people at the heart of everything we do and that this means working to build an inclusive organization in which we reach to include everyone in developing a shared vision and planning how to achieve it.

In Chapter 2, 'The Role of Leadership', I explore the role that leadership must play in building an inclusive organization. I propose that the model of 'traditional leadership' that dominates most organizations is a significant barrier to this change taking place.

I define the nature and parameters of an inclusive organization and the role of a new leadership in building it, and make proposals for an organization-wide programme aimed at developing such an organization which I refer to as 'Creating a New Leadership Initiative'.

Chapter 3, 'The Goals of Transformation', puts the work of building an inclusive organization into the context of our overall approach to organization development. It postulates that leaders will need to pursue three goals if we are to create effective organizations. These are:

O   Managing a turbulent environment;
O   Increasing productivity and quality;
O   Building an inclusive organization.

I further argue that there are three key activities required to enable those goals to be pursued. They are:

O   Developing a shared vision and planning;
O   Adopting the principles of continual improvement and innovation;
O   Eliminating institutional discrimination and prejudice.

Part I shows that where there is an effective process for developing a shared vision and involving people throughout the organization in planning how to achieve it, it becomes possible to look towards managing a turbulent future with some degree of equanimity. In addition, I demonstrate that continual improvement and innovation of every product, service and process will lead to increasing gains in quality and productivity. The concepts of institutional discrimination and prejudice are introduced and it is shown that where there is effective work to eliminate them, it will be possible to build an inclusive organization.

Therefore, I demonstrate that if all three activities are implemented in an integrated and systematic way through effective leadership, an organization can realize the full potential of all of its people in the pursuit of its vision and plans.

1
MAKING SENSE OF THE PRESENT

❖

There is a crisis going on in the world and it is deepening daily. No part of the world is untouched, no organization will survive unless it engages in fundamental change, and no individual can escape its impact however much they hope to remain secure and comfortable. It is an economic, technological, environmental and social crisis and it demands response and action of a different order to any that has been necessary to emerge from previous difficulties that we have faced.

Many of the people now in formal leadership positions, whether in government, in public service organizations or in the private sector, are unable or are not prepared to grasp the scale of the crisis or to face the effects it is having. Apparently they prefer solutions that offer some short-term gain, while leaving the bigger problems to future leaders. Many deny that there is a crisis at all!

Whatever people think or however much they try to pretend that everything is fine, the crisis is happening and it provides us with the most important and exciting challenge of our lives! We are capable of overcoming it, and this book describes some of the actions we will need to take to make that possible. However, to achieve success will require review and change at every level.

THE CRISIS IS PRIMARILY ECONOMIC

The root of the crisis is economic. In a world system driven increasingly by the need to accumulate capital and the constant pursuit of profit, every organization, wherever it is located, is faced with the need to expand its market or reduce its costs, or both, if it is to survive. The competitive imperative dictates that the choice between economic growth or failure is built into the system and as long as the system is constructed in this way, organizations will have to compete.

This has caused a number of contradictions in our economic and social

3

systems and our long-term success or failure depends apparently on our ability to overcome, or at least manage, these contradictions. To begin with, however, let us examime how we arrived at this point.

A LITTLE HISTORY

In the two centuries since the beginning of the Industrial Revolution, competition has taken place primarily on a national basis, with companies within each nation state competing to dominate each sector of the economy. However, during the past 25 years or so, we have moved from a series of national economies – some large and powerful enough to establish a hegemony over others, but most with some degree of independence – to a truly global economic system that is marked by a greater degree of integration and interpenetration across national boundaries than at any previous point in economic history. This new globalized economy is dominated by the tripolar constellation of the United States, Japan and the European Union.

In the developing first world, before 1900 there was not enough capital to fund all of the huge number of projects planned in order to develop a new industrial and social infrastructure, but since the 1900s capital accumulation has been so effective that we have accumulated, on the whole, more capital than we have been able to spend. The effect of this has been to create a supply of funds for loans on a world scale that exceeds the demand for productive investment, and this has caused an underlying economic stagnation. This peaked during the economic collapse of the 1930s.

The need to rebuild after the Second World War, the huge expansion of markets that followed and the creation of the Cold War and its use as justification for massive military expenditure, combined to create the richest period this century, recently referred to as the 'golden age' by Eric Hobsbawm.[1] World leaders and economists assumed that we had solved the problem, but the gradual erosion of the effect of these economic growth factors has led to the reappearance of over-capacity and economic stagnation. Paul Sweezy writes

> More recent events, however, have shown that the burial of stagnation was, to say the least, premature. I hardly need to remind you that by 1970 the problem was back again, this time with a new twist reflected in the name 'stagflation'. This was inevitable because an excess of capital still exists and in recent years this excess has been wasted on a wild orgy of financial speculation, creating an unprecedented situation.[2]

In a way we could say that capital is doing very well while capitalism is doing very badly.

In an effort to overcome this crisis, the past 20 years have seen the reemergence of the old nineteenth century liberal economic *laissez faire* ideology whereby events are left to market forces and this thinking has influenced every aspect of economic activity. It has led to the election of governments throughout the industrialized world who believe that the extension of the market into areas that have previously been the domain of social organization is the best mechanism for improving performance and ensuring economic success in the new global marketplace. This has been accompanied by the wholesale deregulation of financial and market controls and therefore the free flow of capital has enabled an international capital base and a truly global economy to appear for the first time.

CONTRADICTIONS IN THE PRESENT SITUATION

The consequences of these changes are far-reaching. Economic activity in and between the nations of the 'first world' has traditionally been regulated by alliances designed to manage the political and social conflicts that were inherent in the situation, but deregulation means that there is no similar mechanism available today, even between the most developed countries. The General Agreement on Tarifs and Trade (GATT) made during 1994 will only serve to exacerbate the process, although it will affect less developed nations the most.

This situation has been magnified by the fall of the Soviet empire. The sudden entry of a huge command economy on to the world stage with a massive privatization programme requiring an injection of capital bigger than that needed for rebuilding the whole of Europe after the Second World War has added to the turbulence.

As a result, there is dwindling scope for national decisions and we are faced with the widening effects of an autonomous global economy. There is no solution to the problem it raises, since no supranational state is visible on the horizon. This is the first major source of the contradictions that the new globalization is bringing in its train.

In response, a growing tide of nationalist sentiment has appeared, often driven by the desire to recover economic control in the name of national identity. This can take many forms, ranging from the rise of religious fundamentalism as a political force in the United States and in the Middle East, through to the outright opposition to further European integration expressed by some people in the United Kingdom and in other countries. However, the process of global interpenetration is inexorable and the need for world level strategies to manage it will grow in significance.

Alongside this trend comes a second contradiction, namely the position of the countries of the third and fourth world, sometimes called the 'periphery', in relation to the nations of the central tripolar constellation. While, on the one hand, these countries face growing economic failure in their own right, on the other hand they have a role of continuing vital importance in providing natural resources and cheap labour with which the multinational corporations can threaten the workers of the nations of the first world in order to keep wage costs down.

It has gradually become clear that, in order to build a capital base that would enable the world economic system as a whole to move forward, some reallocation of capital will be necessary. However, the adoption of a 'market-orientated' solution to this crisis serves only to exacerbate the difficulties, and is likely to generate growing social, national, and international imbalances that may turn out to be unbearable.

This situation has been compounded by the massive advance of technology into every aspect of our lives. The application of science to every process in order to secure reductions in costs or dominance of the market with new products has increased the rate of change tenfold. Computers, in my lifetime alone, have shrunk in size from occupying whole rooms to sitting in jacket pockets, while the actual costs of purchase have plummeted. If the 1980s saw blue-collar jobs halved in the West by the automation of traditional labour-intensive manual tasks and the transfer of production to the Pacific rim, the 1990s are witnessing white-collar occupations being decimated all over the world by the pursuit of reduced labour costs made possible by the use of technology. The current 'de-layering' of organizations by taking out whole levels of management, often in the name of handing more opportunities to workers at junior levels, has caused widespread redundancies among managers, a group who had been used to a high level of economic security.

Alongside these difficulties is the important question of whether or not we face a full ecological breakdown. The uncontrolled pursuit of economic growth by governments and businesses throughout the world without taking responsibility for the damage done to our environment leads inevitably towards the situation where the planet could be irreparably damaged. It is vital that, at global and regional levels, we adopt policies and programmes that protect the environmental balance. However, this is in complete contradiction to the policies of total deregulation advanced by all the countries of the developed world.

THE SOCIAL DIMENSION

The wholesale adoption of the ideology of the market and the use of market forces and deregulation as a strategy to overcome the crisis by countries such as the United States, Japan and in Europe, has led many governments to the conclusion that their primary role in this new situation is to create what they call an 'enterprise culture'. This new culture emphasizes the importance of people becoming more self-reliant, looking after themselves and their own interests rather than sharing responsibility for the well-being of one another in good times and bad. At the centre of this philosophy is the assumption that people are primarily motivated by money.

This has generally meant a shift towards the importance of material success as the principal criterion for judging one's achievements. The difference in income between the highest and lowest paid has increased dramatically and the position advanced that if you don't succeed it is your own fault. Payment systems have been changed from focusing on fairness and consistency, towards increasing numbers of people being placed on performance-related pay which directly links so-called high performance with higher pay. Top executives are offered valuable stock options, huge salaries and large bonuses which can turn them into extremely wealthy people overnight if their company performs well. For example, large numbers of public corporations have been privatized and the salaries of top managers in them have been doubled and trebled within a year.

At the same time many business leaders and politicians advanced the notion that the pre-eminent problem in the economy was that the trades union movement was too powerful and rafts of legislation have been passed to reduce its power. Many of the traditional methods of protecting workers' interests, such as minimum wage and health and safety legislation, have been eliminated or reduced in the name of building a more competitive economy.

This has led inevitably to political pressures. In many countries in the developed world, where about a third of the population have acquired a good standard of living with some level of economic security, what J.K. Galbraith has called 'a culture of contentment'[3] has grown up. Such people have adopted a 'scarcity mentality' which assumes that opportunities are limited and that, in order to survive, they will need to defend the share they have at present. Some politicians, speaking for these views, have developed programmes aimed at maintaining the status quo politically, economically and socially in favour of them. This has largely meant offering policies of low taxation and high investment in the defence industry.

Since resistance to voting is widespread among the poorest people in these societies, either because of disillusion or to avoid the state knowing their address, members of this advantaged one-third have been able to elect these political parties to power. Consequently, there has been a relative decline in and a continuing pressure to reduce the funds available from the state for infrastructure investment, for health, for education and for social security support, while the level of expenditure on the defence industry skyrocketed in the 1980s.

The effect of this on society as a whole has been that increasing numbers of people throughout the world live below agreed poverty levels, unemployment has levelled out at just under 10 per cent of the population in the developed world and much higher in the less developed world and shows no significant sign of decreasing, and levels of crime and violence are reducing the quality of life for everyone to poorer and poorer levels. Meanwhile, the increasing exposure of corruption among politicians and industrialists has caused a crisis of confidence in the political establishment and a general feeling of disillusion.

PEOPLE AT WORK

The general degradation in working conditions has taken its toll on people's attitudes to work and relationships with one another. People have come to the conclusion that they do not share a common interest with the people with whom they work and this sets them against one another in many different ways. Most people now appreciate that no organization is guaranteed existence and that therefore no job is secure; as a result, morale is low and an underlying climate of fear is common. The elimination of many jobs in the name of cost saving and efficiency has placed huge additional pressures and increasing stress on those

work, be trained or gain promotion in an organization. In an inclusive organization, it is understood that it is necessary to adopt processes that will ensure old patterns of discrimination and prejudice are swept away and that everyone is able to contribute fully regardless of background, race, sex, disability or sexual preference. Processes have to be developed that enable everyone to be involved in deciding the future and improving the functioning of the enterprise.

Building an inclusive organization will therefore require a fundamental change in our consciousness. We will need to develop a passion for involving people in everything that is going on in the organization. We must think and act at all times in such a way as to enhance and add to the long-term quality of the lives of everyone rather than to the short-term interests of particular groups or individuals. We must take positive action to bring everyone into the heart of the enterprise.

To achieve this we shall have to develop a new leadership and a new leadership initiative.

REFERENCES

1.   *Age of Extremes*, Eric Hobsbawm (Michael Joseph, 1994).
2.   *Stagnation and the Financial Explosion*, essays by Harry Magdoff and Paul M. Sweezy (Monthly Review Press, 1987).
3.   *The Culture of Contentment*, John Kenneth Galbraith (Penguin Books, 1993).

2

THE ROLE OF LEADERSHIP

❖

A growing number of leaders have recognized that work to build a new kind of organization is essential if their common enterprise is going to survive and prosper. 'Management and leadership boil down to working with and through people', writes Michael Leadbetter, Director of one of the largest social services departments in the United Kingdom.[1] He continues, 'The best policies, practices and induction programmes are worthless if the people using them are not committed to delivering good services. Failure to work cooperatively and flexibly will lead to services failing users.'

Support for this perspective came from the ground-breaking report produced by the Industrial Society entitled *Blueprint for Success*:[2]

> Committed employees work harder, come up with ideas that the organization can develop, and promote the company to outsiders. That level of enthusiasm cannot be bought. It starts at the top with senior executives walking around, finding out what people think and their interests, and going on to look for ways to provide them with more responsibility, more job interest, and otherwise involving them in the business.[2]

Finally, the much quoted statement from the leading Japanese industrialist Konosuki Makushita in 1985 clearly outlines the issue. Talking about the differences in management practice between Japan, the United States and Europe, he said:

> We are going to win and the industrial West is going to lose. There is nothing much you can do about it, because the reasons for your failure are within yourselves. Your firms are built on the Taylor model; even worse, so are your heads. For you the essence of management is getting the ideas out of the heads of management into the hands of labour. For us, the art of management is mobilizing and pulling together the intellectual resources of all the employees in the service of the firm ... Only by drawing on the combined brainpower of all its employees can a firm face up to the turbulence and constraints of today's environment.[3]

Such executives have begun the arduous but exciting task of developing their

11

own understanding and ability to create a partnership with the people who work in the enterprise. They have launched new initiatives aimed at a fundamental transformation in how their organizations function. This has required the development of a strategy aimed at winning the energy and commitment of people at all levels towards the goals of the organization. It has led them to ask a basic question:

Under what conditions are people most prepared
to give their energy and commitment?

In answering this question, we are all influenced by the fundamental assumptions that we make about what motivates people to contribute fully and thoughtfully. Through much of the 1980s the underlying assumption was that people were primarily motivated by the desire for economic rewards. For example, large numbers of managerial and professional people now receive performance-related pay in the hope of increasing their incentive to perform effectively. Similarly, many sales people have had their basic pay reduced while their income is made up increasingly by commissions generated by sales. As the Performance Appraisal Research Group of the British Deming Association says:

> The spread of performance-related rewards into many areas where they did not previously exist is leading to the hasty introduction of appraisal schemes based on grading and pay. These add to the pressures for short-term results and visibly destroy existing traditions of team-working which have been built up over many years.[4]

I believe that this strategy ultimately leads to the sub-optimization of the work of the organization as a whole. People look after their own interests rather than work towards the success of the whole group. In my work, I assume that people give their energy and commitment most enthusiastically and fully when:

They are valued first and foremost as people and when their thinking and ideas
are encouraged and they then become an integral part of the process of
managing and improving the organization.

This is because I am convinced that people have vastly more potential to contribute than is permitted or encouraged in organizations that have adopted the prevailing ideology of the 1980s and early 1990s. I reject the wholesale reliance on motivation by material advantage because I believe that, while people are very concerned that they are paid fairly and well, their longer-term interest is the desire to be able to contribute, cooperate and do a good job.

This is not a difficult assumption for me to accept. I have always thought that everyone has the capacity for thinking intelligently about the best way to carry out tasks, where I define intelligence as the ability to bring a fresh, new and accurate response to each new situation. I assume that people are able to think creatively, derive new solutions to old problems and have the ability to take the initiative to see that everything goes well and is continually improved. In an environment where people are valued and their thinking encouraged and used, most people will contribute their loyalty, commitment and enthusiasm. In this sense, everyone has the capacity to take leadership.

My reasons for choosing these assumptions are quite simple. First, they fit with research evidence. For example, Frederick Herzberg,[5] first published in the 1960s, demonstrated that people require sufficient funds to be able to meet their basic needs for warmth, shelter and safety, but these are primarily demotivators rather than motivators. They are necessary 'hygiene factors' which inhibit people from giving their best if they are inadequately met. What positively motivates people is the opportunity to develop and use their full potential – achievement, recognition for achievement, intrinsic interest in the work, responsibility and advancement. 'I might add' says Herzberg, 'that many of the barriers to fuller utilization of manpower that are "justified" by economic reasons, are in reality, devices of fearful and inadequate managers who are not prepared to meet the challenges of managing adults.'

Second, these assumptions accord with people's experience of performance-related pay. All current research shows that, when asked, people say they are not primarily motivated by money. Rather, such strategies lead to sub-optimization of performance because people look after their own local interests and not the interests of the organization as a whole. I recall a personnel manager telling me that she had written to the directors of her company offering help to achieve their performance targets, only to be ignored. When she eventually asked one of the directors why he had not replied he said, 'Because if I let you help I won't be able to say I did it myself!'. What a sorry state to be in!

Finally, assuming that people are only motivated by financial incentives leads down a back alley of no hope and no improvement. If we assume that people need to be offered money to give of their best we are stuck with a mean, small-minded approach to one another. The challenge is to obtain the best from people by assuming that they will want to do the very best job possible *because it is the right thing to do*, not because they are being bought to do it.

Such an approach is in complete contradiction to the assumptions and behaviour of much of the management that has been provided in organizations to date. We might call this 'traditional leadership'.

THE 'TRADITIONAL LEADERSHIP' APPROACH

The 'traditional leadership' approach developed originally in different times and for different tasks. The earliest organizational forms appeared in slave societies and progressed to the organization of the army and the church. Even today, most organizations bear an uncanny resemblance to the model developed by the Roman Army. Although we have seen many developments this century in science, technology and communications, we have had less success in applying organizational theory and practice until recent years.

Indeed, the move during the 1980s towards an individualistic and competitive solution to the crisis has exacerbated what were already ingrained traits. Over and over, we have understood the need for something different but we have

It doesn't work!

Clearly, this approach to managing is based upon a set of assumptions and prejudices towards other people that are questionable in the present context. If we take account of the evidence that surrounds us about what motivates people, I propose that we adopt a new philosophy that puts people at the heart of everything we do. Any programme of improvement that does not place people at its centre will simply repeat all the mistakes currently being made in the management of the global and national economies described in Chapter 1, and in most organizations world-wide as described in this chapter. If people are unable to develop and use their full potential they are likely to at the least inhibit and at the most block the organization from achieving its goals.

The challenge is to build the enterprise into an inclusive organization in which everyone is involved, their full potential is liberated, and they are able to contribute a quality of energy and commitment rarely seen when people work under traditional leadership.

WHO IS RESPONSIBLE?

Who is responsible for this work? The radical answer to this question must be that *everyone* is responsible for creating this environment, but for this to happen we must first conceive of everyone in the organization as a potential leader and be prepared to empower them so that they can contribute. While people in formal positions such as managers will need to see themselves as the key leaders of this transformation, the greater challenge is to see people at all levels and in all jobs as providing leadership to the organization where I define leadership as:

> *Working to understand the whole situation and seeing to it that absolutely everything in it goes well, without limit or reservation.*

In this sense, leadership is an attitude of mind, a decision and an activity. It is an attitude towards the world that says, 'I want to learn about and am in charge of absolutely everything no matter how big or small'. It is a decision to see to it that everything goes well and is continually improved. It is putting that attitude and that decision into action everywhere I go. These are the characteristics of the people who have dedicated themselves to building an inclusive organization.

Let me examine the first part of this definition in more detail.

WORKING TO UNDERSTAND THE WHOLE SITUATION

Each of us is the product of how we have been brought up, the particular things that have happened to us, our experience, background and culture. Each of us tends to view the world through the eyes of the people we grew up with, the relationships we have had, the places we have been, and the things that we have been able to do.

We can conceive of this situation as analogous to frying an egg, with each of

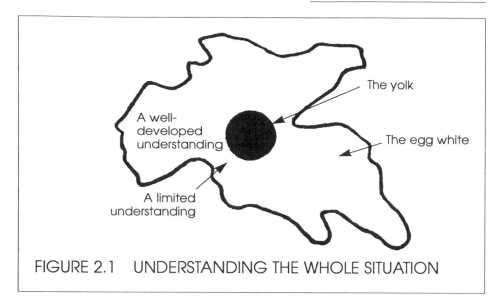

The yolk

A well-developed understanding

The egg white

A limited understanding

FIGURE 2.1   UNDERSTANDING THE WHOLE SITUATION

us the egg yolk and our experience the egg white. As we drop the egg into the hot oil in the frying pan, it will look like the sketch in Figure 2.1. Some parts of the egg white run and are well filled in, whereas, for whatever reason, other areas do not run at all. Similarly, as leaders, there are some things that we know a great deal about and can handle well and there are others in which we have had less experience and will be less able to think about and manage well.

Moreover, there is a strong tendency for most of us to reduce any situation to something that we can comprehend within the limits of our own experience so as to reduce the level of uncertainty, rather than dealing with it in its true complexity. Sometimes, in order to try to make sense of events, we adopt a prejudiced attitude or accept a negative stereotype towards other people or events, but this reduces our openness and ability to understand the situation.

Consequently, our appreciation and understanding become somewhat limited. Therefore, if we are to understand more of the whole situation, we will have to begin by accepting that we do not have a complete picture and that we will need continually to extend our view if we are to function effectively. I find it helps to imagine ourselves as apprentices, in the certain knowledge that we will never become a master. We will travel through life learning more by consciously making the effort to expand the limited 'appreciation' that each of us has of the world around us including the effects of our own behaviour on those things.

Of course, no one will ever understand everything that is happening! Leading well does not require that we understand everything, since this is impossible. As long as we accept that we don't understand everything and providing that we continually strive to understand as much of the whole picture as possible, we can relax. After all, other people know about many of the aspects that we do not know about and our challenge is to enable them to play a full part. If their

In doing this well, we will make every effort to treat the people around us with respect, support and encouragement. We will set up situations where we are able to draw out their best ideas and thinking. We will create the conditions that enable them to contribute their full intelligence, work together towards shared goals, and form effective, close working relationships with one another; thus, we become leaders of leaders rather than leaders of followers.

A vital component in building an inclusive organization will be to guarantee equality of opportunity for those people who have been traditionally subject to prejudice and negative stereotypes about their abilities, such as women, black people, people with disabilities and younger people.

TRANSFORMING THE ORGANIZATION

The primary role of leadership is to transform the organization. Top management has a special responsibility for this process. Control of the culture and climate in a hierarchical organization, as of the construction of the system itself, is always strongly influenced by the behaviour of the most senior people, the chief executive and his or her team. It is therefore their responsibility to communicate that they are putting people at the centre and to develop policies and practices for involving them at all levels. They have to know what is really going on in the organization, know what people think, have greater expectations of them, look for ways to involve them, cherish their contribution, and develop their self-confidence and abilities. Top management needs to model this for middle and junior management, setting goals that will create a shift in this direction.

For people without a formal leadership position or who are in a junior role in the organization, it also means a fundamental change that carries big responsibilities. They must claim the power that is on offer, put their understandable cynicism to one side, and work with managers at more senior levels to build the new organization. They must adopt the notion that they too are leaders and join with others in working to understand the whole situation and seeing to it that everything goes well.

I believe we must apply these ideas and viewpoints about leadership across the whole organization as part of a process of total organizational transformation. When people at all levels strive to include one another, begin to take their power and see themselves as colleague leaders in a joint endeavour I call it 'creating a new leadership initiative'. The organization is energized, people feel valued and included and ready to go!

Creating a new leadership initiative will require an organization-wide programme designed to develop the awareness and skills of people at all levels so that they are able to inspire, encourage and lead one another to contribute the best of their thinking and to take the initiative to promote transformation. I describe this programme in Chapter 14.

I have set out the key challenge to the manager – to become a leader who is working to understand the whole situation and deciding to see to it that absolutely everything in it goes well. In the next chapter I turn to the key activities that are needed to make a fundamental improvement in the performance of the organization.

REFERENCES

1. 'The Best Job in the World', Michael Leadbetter (*Care Weekly*, 24 February 1994).
2. *Blueprint for Success*, The Industrial Society (1990).
3. Quoted by Roger Smith at the International Conference of Personnel Management, 1985.
4. *Performance Appraisal and All That!* British Deming Association Performance Appraisal Research Group (1991).
5. *The Motivation to Work*, Frederick Herzberg (John Wiley and Sons, 1959).

3

THE GOALS OF TRANSFORMATION

The challenge is to begin to implement policies and strategies that put people at the heart of everything we do, whether they are customers or employees. This means developing strategies that reach to include everyone in the enterprise in planning and deciding upon the future direction of the business and in contributing to the continual improvement of how it functions. When people are excluded they feel marginalized and left out, their morale suffers and they are unable to give their best to the organization.

I call this process 'organizational transformation'. It must be aimed, in my view, at three goals. These are:

O   Managing the future in a turbulent environment;
O   Improving productivity and quality;
O   Building an inclusive organization.

MANAGING THE FUTURE IN A TURBULENT ENVIRONMENT

The emergence of the global economy and the accompanying mounting international competition have produced a turbulent environment much as Eric Trist predicted in his 1965 paper, 'The Causal Texture of Organizational Environments'.[1] Trist wrote that the emergence of a turbulent environment would produce trends which would bring with them a 'gross increase in unpredictability for corporations and individuals alike'. He continued: 'What becomes precarious under these conditions is how organizational stability can be achieved. In these environments individual organizations, however large, cannot expect to adapt successfully simply through their own direct actions.'

This has resulted in a huge increase in anxiety for people at all levels of the organization. As people become more fearful, they maintain a low profile and limit their contribution to the minimum necessary. This situation cannot be resolved without management understanding the importance of involving people at every level of the enterprise in planning how to manage the future. People

23

need to understand and 'appreciate' what is happening, feel a part of the process for managing it, and share a unifying sense of direction to guide them through the uncertainty. Creating the opportunity for people to contribute their thinking about where the organization is heading has become an essential component of effective organizational management if we wish to manage the future effectively.

IMPROVING PRODUCTIVITY AND QUALITY

Improving productivity and quality in the delivery of products and services has become a priority for any enterprise to survive in the world of international competition. People, as customers, are increasingly exercising their judgement about the products and services they buy, and they favour only those that are of the very highest standard. Moreover, every corporation throughout the world is looking systematically at how to produce 'more for less', and, therefore, finding ways of making substantial improvements in productivity is a necessity for everyone.

Thus, improving products and processes has become an imperative if organizations are to aspire to the title of 'world class'. This means working systematically to develop a practice that will enable them to achieve that level of performance.

BUILDING AN INCLUSIVE ORGANIZATION

The most important asset remaining untapped in many organizations is the huge reservoir of ability in its people. It is apparent that many corporations continue to exclude people from the opportunity to take leadership and contribute fully towards the goals of the organization. This situation has been tackled with some success through programmes designed to increase equality of opportunity for many groups, in particular women, black people and people with disabilities, though much remains to be done. However, we now have a new problem – regardless of how well these programmes have succeeded in reality, this process has led people who are not in those groups to begin to feel left out, and a backlash has begun.

We must now reach for yet a higher level of functioning. We must begin to build an inclusive organization. This means taking positive action to bring everybody into every aspect of the work of the enterprise. It means welcoming people with all their diversity of backgrounds and abilities because they add a value to performance that those who 'fit' the existing profile of people in the organization are unable to offer. They are not 'safe' but they bring excitement and energy and new competencies into the heart of the business.

TRANSFORMING THE ORGANIZATION

The three *goals of transformation* are shown in graphic form in Figure 3.1. We begin the process by developing leaders who are working to understand the whole situation and deciding to see to it that absolutely everything goes well.

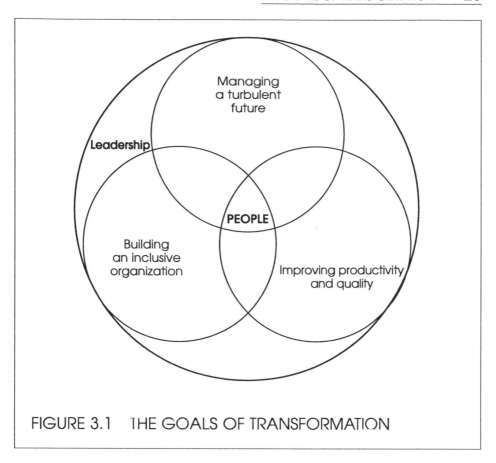

FIGURE 3.1   THE GOALS OF TRANSFORMATION

Such leaders put people at the centre, whether they are customers or employees. They work to achieve the goals of transformation through the effective application of leadership to the process at all levels.

THE THREE ACTIVITIES

In pursuing these goals, leaders will focus their organization on three key activities (illustrated in Figure 3.2). These activities are:

O   Enabling everyone in the enterprise to develop a shared vision of the future and planning how to achieve it.
O   Developing a culture of innovation and continual improvement towards all products, services and processes.
O   Taking positive action to enable everyone at all levels to contribute their full potential towards the shared vision and their own work.

The practice of developing a shared vision and plans enables the enterprise to manage a turbulent future. Continual improvement and innovation enables the

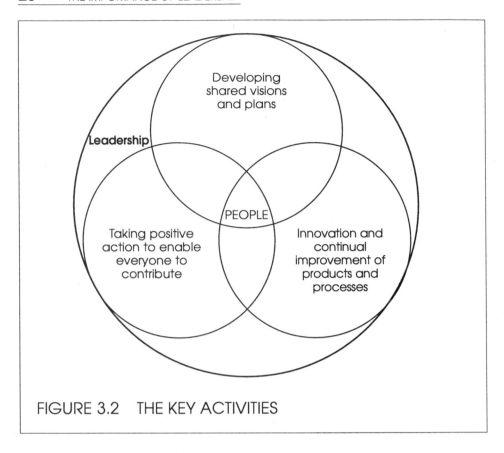

FIGURE 3.2   THE KEY ACTIVITIES

enterprise to improve quality and productivity. Taking positive action to enable everyone to contribute enables the enterprise to build an inclusive organization.

In the context of this book, it is the third activity – taking positive action to enable everyone to contribute – that is the most important. However, on its own it would still not be sufficient to guarantee success. Work is needed in all three areas and if these are thoughtfully integrated then different but interacting contributions will be made to the effectiveness of the organization.

DEVELOPING A SHARED VISION AND PLANNING

Any organization faced with a turbulent environment needs a clear vision of the direction it is taking, and plans for reaching that vision. These activities enable people to review and 'appreciate' their present situation, develop a common description of where they would like to be, based on what they value and believe is important, and then work together to agree their plans. In a world of uncertainty, this brings some sense of purpose, of knowing where things are going and how best to get there, and this reduces ambiguity and offers direction.

It is my view that most senior managers have grasped the importance of developing a clear vision, but, to the extent that they are 'trapped' in traditional leadership, they still think the next step is to 'sell' it to people at more junior levels. I recommend finding ways to involve everyone in the organization in undertaking this work. In saying this, I am assuming the following:

O   Everyone is capable of making a relevant and useful contribution to the vision building and planning process.
O   People will be more likely to make plans work or be agreeable to changing them should the need arise if they have been involved in their development.
O   This not only produces better plans but reduces anxiety and conflict so that success is more likely.

When we involve people we make possible an improvement in how people see themselves, increasing their sense of worth and self-esteem. If we adopt a process that enables everyone in the enterprise to contribute, people feel valued and more committed to achieving the planned outcomes.

The business planning process itself offers one of the best opportunities for a common enterprise to include people from all levels and thereby become truly accessible to its members. Clarifying and agreeing the vision, strategies, and detailed action plans for the future should be an iterative process involving people at every level and in every activity. This can be done in a series of steps taken over time, as follows:

O   The top team develops an initial vision statement and then cascades this to the next level with the request that people examine it and then undertake their own vision building. They then pass their vision back to the top group.
O   The top group integrates all of the visions generated into one overall vision and begins planning for how to move forward over the next period. These plans are cascaded to the next level for examination with the request to build their own plans. These sub-group plans are then passed back to the top team.
O   The top team then integrates all of these plans and develops the overall 'enterprise plan'.

It is possible over a number of years to increase the number of levels engaged in this process so that eventually everyone is working on the vision and making plans. The vision building and planning process has then become a central part of the functioning of the enterprise in its own right, guiding its direction and involving the whole organization in the work.

However, despite the care taken to involve people in the process described above, such approaches for introducing change still founder on a lack of thoroughgoing commitment from some individuals, from certain departments or from different levels. A radical approach to this problem involves getting all of the key people together in a room (as many as 2,000 people have been reported in one organization) and working with them on diagnosing the present situation, developing a collective vision of how they would like it to be and planning a strategy together for how to achieve it. This gets all of the right people together at one time, gives them all an opportunity to contribute and binds their commitment to the outcomes and decisions made. It can be applied to many different issues such as developing a collective vision, developing a strategy for change, or planning restructuring – all perfect targets for such activities.

There are detailed descriptions of the specific steps involved in developing a vision of the future and how to plan in Chapter 10.

ADOPTING THE PRINCIPLES AND PRACTICE OF CONTINUAL IMPROVEMENT AND INNOVATION

Many people in formal leadership positions such as managers still spend their lives either taking instructions and trying to please the boss upstairs, or fire-fighting, whereby they hope against hope that one day, despite their reactive mode, they will be able to catch up. Today, we are in a new era in which we expect people, as leaders, to decide to see to it that absolutely everything goes well and keeps improving. It is apparent, however, that people do not actually know how to improve the effectiveness of a system, otherwise they would do so. Therefore, this requires the systematic education and development of people throughout the organization on how to undertake continual process improvement.

I begin by assuming that any organization of people working together is a system with a central purpose or mission. It comprises a number of processes

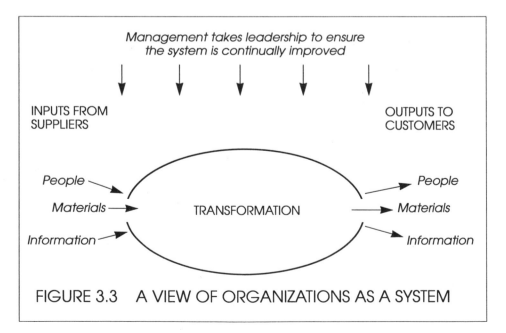

FIGURE 3.3   A VIEW OF ORGANIZATIONS AS A SYSTEM

commencing at one end with the input of people, materials and information which are then transformed into some new output at the other end, as shown in Figure 3.3.

The challenge is to optimize the performance of the system in relation to the needs of its customers. This means a profound shift of understanding about the importance of the people the organization serves. Traditionally customers and clients have been seen as something outside of the organization to be 'tolerated' but not really central to people's thinking about the purpose of their work. The inclusive organization values every possible customer, and its goal is to reach customers it has not traditionally served by exceeding their minimum expectations and ensuring that they are completely delighted with the product or service received.

This concept can be applied also to relationships between people inside the organization. Thinking of oneself as a customer, or supplier of products or services to colleagues, is new for many people; but achieving delighted customers is as important between 'suppliers' and 'customers' inside the organization as it is for those outside. Taking on this perspective leads to an attitude of responsibility for one's own performance and respect for the person one is supplying or from whom one receives supplies.

The next step is to ensure that the purpose or mission of the organization is clearly defined and its sub-processes clearly identified. Any system that does not have a clear statement of its aim is open to misdirection and it is difficult to monitor its performance if there is nothing to monitor it against.. The organization draws up flow-charts describing its own process and uses the charts to develop customer focus and to enable people to engage in systematic improvement activities.

Installing the practice of continual improvement requires an understanding of variation in system performance and a knowledge of techniques for optimizing the performance of the organization as a whole by focusing in depth on the causes of variation. This includes deciding whether a problem is a temporary deviation due to causes that are inherent within the system, or a difficulty which is caused by special circumstances, which indicates that the system is out of control. The first step is to bring the system into control and then proceed to study systematically how to develop its performance as a process.

People also need to learn how to base their decisions and improvements upon real knowledge rather than opinion. Decisions are always based upon a prediction about what will happen if we take this or that action, and it is important that people adopt a systematic approach to the process of continual improvement. I recommend working through the PDSA (Plan–Do–Study–Act) cycle which involves planning (P), implementing the plan (D), studying the results (S) and then standardizing the changes across the organization (A) based on what we have learnt and/or recycling into a revised improvement plan.

The practice of continual improvement needs to take over the organization, with people at every level and across levels and functions being involved in meetings to review performance, investigate variation and agree detailed action plans. The result will be a fundamental and sustained improvement in the quality of processes, products and services, and it will have been created by everyone.

Continual involvement on its own is not enough. The organization has to ensure that it is continually innovative in developing its products, services and processes. For example, manufacturing the best carburettor in the world would still leave us out of business if competitors have developed electronic ignition and it takes over the marketplace. Creating an environment in which we are able to make big leaps in how we make products, deliver services, or in the products or services themselves, demands patience and investment but leads to truly delighted customers.

TAKING POSITIVE ACTION TO ENABLE EVERYONE TO CONTRIBUTE

The most important blockages to people being able to contribute lie in the effects of discrimination and prejudice. Every person in an enterprise is affected, and work to eliminate them is essential to any programme aimed at increasing the effectiveness of the organization, as well as making a contribution towards improving the working life of every person involved. Discrimination and prejudice aimed at any individual or group of people using the excuse of their gender, race, disability, or any other aspect of their identity is, in my opinion, the biggest single reason for the waste of human potential and the under-utilization of people's thinking and abilities in most enterprises, and in society as a whole. Discrimination and prejudice systematically prohibits people from contributing and damage people's sense of self-worth and confidence, and therefore their willingness to take themselves and their contribution seriously.

A common but mistaken assumption is that this issue only concerns the treatment of 'minorities'; but, as I will demonstrate later in the book, discrimination directly affects most people – women, black people, disabled people, people of all classes, older people, younger people, people of particular religions and people from different regions. It also affects men, parents and single people. This covers the majority of people in most organizations and in fact many people are discriminated against in a number of ways because they 'belong' to several groups.

Claiming to treat everyone equally is not enough because this ignores people's different starting points that result from historical inequalities. We must, then, strategize how to release the vast potential of the majority of people in the organization who have been traditionally under-valued and under-utilized. This will only be achieved if we adopt a positive approach designed to help undo the effects of past discrimination on people who are subject to prejudice. Work with people holding prejudicial attitudes will also be necessary to develop their ability to become 'leaders for equality' and to eliminate the possibility of further mistreatment.

The ultimate challenge is to enlist everyone's help to build an inclusive organization. The whole organization should develop an obsession with 'getting involved', bringing people in, welcoming and embracing diversity, and empowering people to take charge. Rather than the traditional grey uniformity, people will look and act differently, but one thing they will all have in common is a shared vision and commitment to improvement.

INTEGRATING THE THREE KEY ACTIVITIES

To achieve a successful transformation we have to integrate the three key activities into an overall strategy. The key to this lies in people in formal leadership positions acting to release the real potential of people by involving them fully in the enterprise. As I said at the beginning of this chapter, the act of leadership is the integrating factor which fuses all of these activities together. A profound understanding of the whole situation and the decision to see to it that absolutely everything goes well places people at the centre of everything and then ensures the effective application of the three key activities to the enterprise.

Many people would still say that to achieve this situation is not possible. Although the artificially contrived conflict between the needs of the business and the needs of people was demolished many years ago, there is still a considerable time lag in practice. However, when the three activities are integrated effectively, they constitute a practical programme for meeting the needs of the enterprise to be successful while at the same time meeting the needs of the individual to be included, powerful, intelligent and creative.

The activities are linked by a number of common threads which have to be drawn together. Perhaps the most important is the decision to put people at the centre of everything we do, but a second common thread lies in the way that processes and procedures need to be developed. None of the areas can be tacked on to an enterprise as an optional extra; they have minimal value as separate 'add-on' initiatives. They need to be integrated into the infrastructure and operation of the enterprise as a system in an ongoing way. It is only when they are integrated into the culture of the organization as a whole that they really have a chance to work.

A third common thread is the emphasis on cooperation rather than competition. It has been said that one reason attempts to improve quality have been more successful in Japan than in Western countries is because the Japanese have a profound understanding of the importance of cooperation, while Europeans and Americans have been raised in a culture of competition and aggressive individualism. Implementing the three activities requires people to think all of the time about how to cooperate and work together towards a common end.

When each activity is implemented fully and the three activities are fully integrated through effective leadership a synergy occurs between each of the activities and the people in the enterprise that leads to a number of powerful and exciting outcomes, which include the following:

O   A culture in which people know where they are going and have real enthusiasm and commitment.

○   The empowerment of people to take their full part in improving the performance of the enterprise and be recognized and valued accordingly for that contribution.

○   The full involvement of people who have been traditionally excluded at all levels and in all occupations and process.

○   A fundamental improvement in the quality of products, processes and services so that the customer is delighted.

This book is primarily about the relationship between leadership and one of these key activities, eliminating institutional discrimination and prejudice. Part II explores the inherent nature of human beings, the systematic mistreatment of people because of their membership of particular groups, what happens to women and men, and what needs to be done.

REFERENCE

1. 'The Causal Texture of Organizational Environments', Eric Trist (Human Relations, 1965, **18**, 21–31).

PART II
DEVELOPING WOMEN AND MEN AS LEADERS

❖

M any years ago I listened to the closing speaker at a conference of consultants and trainers discussing leadership. He spoke for over an hour about research he had undertaken into the personality characteristics of effective leaders, and, as he described a number of traits, it gradually dawned on me that, in reality, he was talking about men. As he continued, I felt increasingly outraged that he was unaware of the influence of sexism in his research and I wondered how the women in the audience must feel, as they were effectively excluded.

This key event encouraged me to study and explore more about the effects of sexism on men's and women's leadership. I began by examining whether there are inherent differences between women and men. Clearly, genetic background has an impact on our abilities, but I assume it becomes interwoven with the effects of experience, and it is the effects of how people are brought up and the effects of their experience in organizations that we are able to influence. While it is not possible to influence the genetic make-up of a person after the event, any damage that is done as a consequence of experience must, logically, be capable of being undone.

I have tried to bring all of this thinking together in Part II. I describe the key assumptions and understanding that can guide our thinking about how to develop effective leadership for women and men working together in a common enterprise. These include hypotheses about the inherent nature of human beings and the effect of oppression on how people function. I examine the effects of gender conditioning on women and men and make proposals for the specific work that each group will need to do in order to develop an effective leadership.

Chapter 4, 'On Being Human', provides an introduction to my basic assumptions about human beings, and a description of how their ability to function becomes damaged by accident, contagion and oppression, and the implications for people's ability to lead. I introduce the concept of 'contradiction' as the key to recovery from the effects of this damage.

Chapter 5, 'How Oppression Damages Leadership Potential', comprises an introduction to the way in which institutionalized discrimination and prejudice towards the members of particular groups limit the opportunity and ability of individuals to lead effectively.

Chapter 6, 'Undermining Women's Leadership', offers an introduction to the effects of sexism upon women at work and in their personal lives, both in terms of institutionalized discrimination and prejudice. I describe how women internalize sexism and the effect this has on their leadership.

Chapter 7 is called 'Challenging Internalized Sexism' and in it I detail a number of steps women could take to counteract the effects of internalized sexism on their leadership.

In Chapter 8, 'Understanding Men's Gender Conditioning', I suggest that there is an oppression of men and I describe the effects of 'gender conditioning' on men and their leadership.

Chapter 9, 'Developing a New Leadership for Men', offers an introduction to the changes in attitudes and behaviour that men will need to adopt if they are to develop an effective leadership practice. I propose that men will need to claim their vulnerability and I examine what it would mean if men were to give up control in their interpersonal relationships with women and their monopoly of institutional power.

4

ON BEING HUMAN

❖

A s I have developed my work with organizations over the past 25 years, it has become clear to me that most people are unable to provide the kind of leadership needed to build an inclusive organization. It was apparent that, before I would be able to propose a successful strategy for developing leaders, I would first need to explain why people behave in the way they do, given the overwhelming need for something more effective. Why do people not only function less well than they are able to, but also often behave in irrational ways?

When I examined my experience, it seemed to me that the fundamental difficulty lies in the damage done by the physical and emotional 'hurts' that people receive during their lives, especially if they are unable to recover from these hurts. Over time the hurts accumulate and then interfere with their ability to think and operate effectively and powerfully.

I have identified two particular ways in which people are hurt and their ability to lead is undermined; the first is through mistreatment as an individual and the second is the result of mistreatment by society.

In the latter case, people may be mistreated as a result of institutional discrimination and prejudice aimed at them because of their membership of a particular group. On the one hand, they are denied the opportunity to lead, while, on the other hand, members of other groups are promoted to leadership, particularly if they conform with the requirements of the organizational culture as it is presently established. This limits the opportunity and ability of both groups, including the 'successful' group, to provide effective, thoughtful leadership. I use the term 'oppression' to describe this process.

In Chapter 5, I explore the nature of oppression and its effects on the ability of people to lead, by examining how institutional discrimination and prejudice operate in our organizations and damage everyone's leadership. First, however, I shall examine how we are hurt as individuals and I make proposals about the following:

WE ARE INHERENTLY ZESTFUL

This characteristic describes our attitude to life and being alive. I assume that we are zestful, that we naturally love life, are optimistic, enthusiastic and completely hopeful. We are not inherently pessimistic or cynical about the world or other people. For example, young people are generally excited about learning, curious as can be, and thrilled to be alive.

An important corollary to this, for leaders and organizations, is to understand that we are not naturally resistant to change. I believe it is inherent in our nature to welcome every situation as an opportunity to learn. When people around us are positive, encouraging, full of high expectations and accept that mistakes are quite normal, we human beings are open to learning new things and enormously flexible.

WE ARE INHERENTLY COOPERATIVE

A second characteristic describes our relationship to one another. I assume that we are inherently cooperative. Our real nature is to delight in one another and to thoroughly enjoy collaborating together for the resolution of common problems. We are not inherently competitive, domineering, submissive or full of other bad feelings towards one another.

WE ARE INHERENTLY COMPLETELY POWERFUL

A third characteristic is that we are all inherently completely powerful. This should not be confused with traditional concepts of power, which generally focus on domination and submission. I assume that we would naturally take full charge of our work and be completely committed to doing an excellent job. We would not tolerate anyone, including ourselves, being treated with anything less than complete respect even for a moment.

WE ARE ALL EAGER TO LEARN

I assume that we are now and have always been eager to learn. Very young children are thoroughly curious and learn at an extraordinary rate. When my children transferred to secondary school aged 11, they were enormously excited and enthusiastic about the new challenges and learning ahead of them. The young workers I meet during their first days in an organization have high hopes of success, of learning and of making a contribution. In all of these situations that initial excitement disappears within a few years and sometimes within just a few months, yet people remain as enthusiastic to learn as ever when the conditions are right.

All of the research on young people and people at work indicates that the most effective learning takes place in a climate of high expectations and appreciation. We learn best when told we are doing well, that we are liked and thought to be capable of doing well.

WE ARE ALL NATURAL LEADERS

As an integral part of being intelligent, zestful, cooperative, powerful and eager to learn, I assume that every single one of us is capable of taking leadership, where leadership is defined as working to understand the whole situation and deciding to see to it that absolutely everything goes well. I assume that this ability is widely spread through the population, and not in any way limited to a narrow group of people on the basis of gender, class background, colour or any other classification.

THIS IS NOT HOW MOST PEOPLE BEHAVE!

However, it is clear these assumptions are not borne out in practice. Something happens to turn us into people who are much more limited in our capabilities than we should expect to be the case if our inherent nature is as I have described it.

The most cogent explanation for what happens to us is, simply, that we get 'hurt'. A 'hurt' is anything experienced by or done to a person which is not congruent with or reflective of her or his inherent human nature. Obviously, getting 'hurt' physically always hurts – first we are surprised because we don't expect it to happen, and then the 'pain' of the hurt itself follows. However, being treated in any way as less than a full human being also hurts. Perhaps this is the best argument in favour of this optimistic view of our inherent nature – if our nature is not intelligent, zestful, cooperative and powerful, why does it hurt so much to be treated as less than that?

DIFFERENT KINDS OF HURTS

We can be hurt in many different ways but these can be categorized into three basic kinds. They are hurts caused:

O   *By Accident:* We can be hurt by the effects of an accident – for example, we fall off our bicycle or we are under the wrong volcano at the wrong time. Whatever the cause, we assume that human intervention could not have made any difference, and getting hurt at that time was 'inevitable'.

O   *By Contagion:* We can be hurt by the way in which people around us behave or treat us as an individual – I call this being hurt by 'contagion'. For example, simply being with people who are hurting and who are not behaving well as a consequence can hurt us, especially if we don't understand what is going on. Our mothers, fathers and teachers have been hurt themselves, and then with the very best of intentions, they hurt us, and this is passed on generation to generation, rather like a contagious disease.

O   *By Oppression:* Finally, we can be hurt as a consequence of the way discrimination and prejudice are systematically structured into our society (to be examined more fully in Chapter 5).

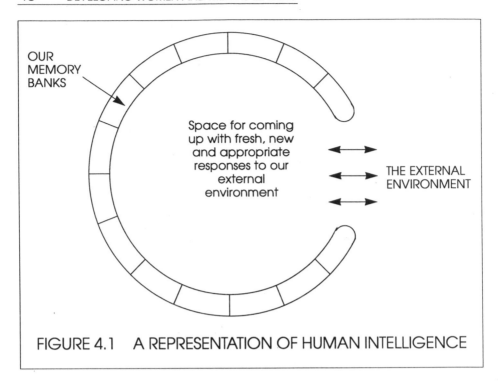

OUR MEMORY BANKS

Space for coming up with fresh, new and appropriate responses to our external environment

THE EXTERNAL ENVIRONMENT

FIGURE 4.1   A REPRESENTATION OF HUMAN INTELLIGENCE

In order to examine the effects of getting hurt upon how we function, it is useful to begin with a representation of how our intelligence works when it is not under any stress or tension. In diagrammatic form it would operate as portrayed in Figure 4.1.

We are engaged with and completely connected to our environment. We use our huge capacity for making fresh, new and appropriate responses to handle each situation. This capacity is based on our ability to think afresh, to compare and contrast our present situation with the huge amount of information stored in our memory banks at incredibly rapid speed, and then to come up with an appropriate, flexible and elegant response.

WE HAVE A NATURAL RECOVERY PROCESS

With this concentration on how we get hurt, it would be understandable for you to think that this is all bad news! However, the complex process of human evolution seems to have provided us with a natural process which, under ideal conditions, allows us to recover completely from the emotional effects of any hurtful experience. If this process is allowed to take place in a relaxed and supportive atmosphere, we are apparently able to continue to function congruently with our inherent nature. If it is not, then we have to adapt our behaviour in ways that leave us looking as though we do not possess that nature after all. Figure 4.2 shows this recovery process.

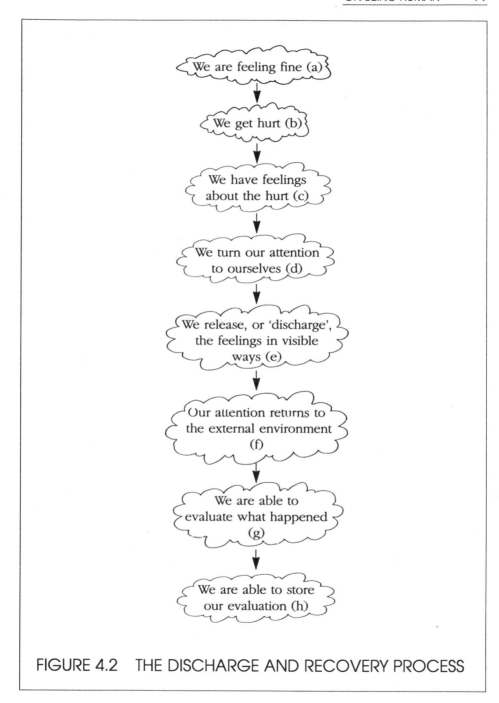

FIGURE 4.2   THE DISCHARGE AND RECOVERY PROCESS

We start out feeling fine (a). Then something happens that 'hurts' us (b). It could be the result of an accident, such as falling off our bicycle, or perhaps we are mistreated in some way by the people around us because of misinformation or prejudice towards us.

When we are hurt we need to 'feel' and 'release' the feelings we have (c). Sometimes this is acceptable – for example, 'have a good cry, it will do you good' is said often enough. At this point it is as though we are disconnected from our environment and turn our attention to ourselves (d). Our intelligence is still functioning, but it is working to help us deal with the painful emotions we are feeling rather than engaging with the world.

I call the process of 'releasing' the feelings, 'discharge' (e). Discharge is the reliable manifestation of healing the emotional distresses and recovering from the hurt. Once we have had sufficient opportunity to discharge – what is 'sufficient' obviously depends on how big the hurt is – our intelligence and attention returns to the external environment (f). We are then able to evaluate what has happened (g) and store the insights gained in the appropriate part of our memory banks for future comparison and contrast when we next need to come up with a fresh new and appropriate response (h).

DISCHARGE AND RECOVERY

As human beings we experience many kinds of feelings, both good and bad. Apparently, each of the 'bad' feelings relates to particular kinds of hurts. Some of the most important are the following:

O   *Loss:* People experience some kind of loss every day. Of course there are big losses when someone dies, but there are many other kinds of losses that can hurt deeply. Losing a wallet or, worse, having it stolen, bumping the car, missing the train or failing an examination. Being treated as having less than one's real ability is a big loss and always hurts.

O   *Embarrassment:* We tend to forget how acutely painful embarrassment was for us when we were teenagers. The fear or experience of ridicule and teasing makes everyone fearful, and while it may not be completely disabling it can be very painful.

O   *Fear:* Being frightened is a very important feeling. Many young people are brought up with fear in the home or in school and in organizations that are dominated by traditional leadership and still tend to use fear as a motivator. Eliminating blame, criticism and attack are vital if people are to feel safe to contribute their best thinking and efforts.

O   *Righteous indignation:* People become angry when they are mistreated. In a small child this may take the form of a temper tantrum, but many adults become furious when they are thwarted.

O   *Boredom:* This is a much under-rated hurt. Many of us spent hours during our youth being thoroughly bored sitting in front of teachers who were not really interested in us, or we have been stuck in work situations that did not test our ability. A common response is to tune out and retreat inside, but being bored is still a very painful experience.

Our ability to recover from these hurtful experiences and the feelings that

Painful emotion or feeling	The reliable symptom of healing – discharge
Grief, loss, feeling alone and abandoned, invalidation and put down	Tears, crying, sobbing
Embarrassment, teasing, ridicule	Giggling and warm perspiration
Fear, humiliation, terror	Shaking and cold perspiration
Righteous indignation, frustration, anger	A 'whoosh' of loud angry noises; a temper tantrum
Boredom	Laughter, animated and interested talking

• •

Physical stresses, tensions and injuries	Yawning and stretching

FIGURE 4.3   THE RECOVERY PROCESS IN ACTION

follow can become manifest in many ways, assuming that the situation encourages and supports the discharge of emotions. Figure 4.3 illustrates the recovery process, by identifying the major areas of painful emotions and the reliable symptom of healing of each.

Different situations make it more or less possible for people to discharge when there is a need to. For example, in the workplace people often talk about their difficulties with one another and this itself is of great value, but only rarely are people able to let their deeper feelings show.

Before proceeding to the next section here is a further word about the discharge of anger. Much of what people consider to be anger is not. Anger discharges with a rapid 'whoosh', a short temper tantrum, and then the person recovers and feels fine. Much of the violence and aggression we generally associate with anger is really a recording of fear, 'dramatizing' or being acted out much as it was acted out on the young person when they first recorded it.

AN EXPLANATION FOR HUMAN IRRATIONALITY

Every society develops its own culture and a crucial part of it is the attitude people are brought up to take towards the expression of feelings. Despite the importance of discharge to the recovery from hurt and the functioning of our intelligence, the recovery process is systematically inhibited in all societies – first, by other people and subsequently, as the person 'internalizes' the inhibition, by the person concerned. While it is always inhibited for both women and men it

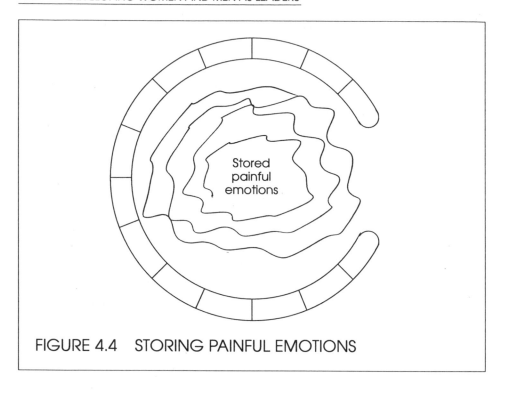

Stored painful emotions

FIGURE 4.4   STORING PAINFUL EMOTIONS

is usually inhibited in particular ways for each sex – women, for example, being allowed to cry a little more and men being permitted to get angry.

It seems to me that this inhibition is partly caused by a profound misunderstanding. All societies throughout history appear to have confused the process of recovery, which would naturally follow the hurt, with the hurt itself. So, for example, we imagine that when someone cries, this is a symptom of that person being hurt, when, in fact, the person has already been hurt and crying is a symptom of the person beginning to deal with the feelings that result from the hurt by using the recovery process. The process of discharge is so central to human recovery, that I believe that not being allowed to discharge might well be the biggest hurt of all.

When discharge is interfered with, the inherent healing process stops and we are unable to recover from the effects of the hurtful experience. However, we still make a recording, but instead of storing our understanding of the event in our memory banks, we make a recording of the painful experience itself and store the feelings along with what is usually incorrect information. This is stored not in the memory banks (see Figure 4.4), but in the 'space' normally used for working out fresh, new and appropriate responses. It is like a growing pile of logs that takes up the space needed for flexible, intelligent functioning. It remains there, a piece of undischarged painful emotion or 'distress recording', waiting for the opportunity to be discharged, but in the meantime, reducing and limiting the ability of the person to function well.

Moreover, we don't get hurt only once in our lives. We 'fall off our bicycle' many times and, as we learn to stifle the discharge that should follow spontaneously, we soon accumulate many similar distress recordings from various accidents and other hurtful experiences.

THE DEVELOPMENT OF CHRONIC COPING PATTERNS

Since much of the way in which we are hurt is a product of misinformation or prejudice on someone else's part, it is likely that we will be hurt in the same way over and over again. For example, some young people are told repeatedly that they are stupid and lazy and each time prohibited from discharging the painful feelings that result. In a way this is inevitable, because if the people we are with most when we are young behave in a particular way once, they are very likely to behave that way again, and so we are almost bound to adopt the behaviour too.

However, this is not the end of the story. Even though we continue to accumulate undischarged distresses, we still have to survive in what we probably experience as a hostile world, and so we begin to adapt our nature to fit with the way the world seems to require us to be. You could say that we 'internalize' the hurts. We develop ways of coping with events, and this soon becomes a 'chronic pattern' of behaviour. I use the word 'chronic' in the medical sense – hence, a cold is an 'acute illness' because it comes briefly and then leaves, while arthritis is a 'chronic illness' because it is a condition which is present all of the time. Chronic coping patterns are rigid responses, like inflexible scar tissue around an old injury, limiting our view of ourselves and our ability to handle the world effectively. I illustrate these in Figure 4.5 as though they form a new skin growing on the outside of our human nature.

Consequently, it is very probable that even the best functioning person in this society is using only some 10 per cent of her or his actual intelligence. The other 90 per cent is locked up in undischarged painful emotion.

Chronic patterns might include such deep-seated attitudes as 'You can't trust anyone else!', 'I'm not good enough' or 'People always leave me out!'. They also include all of the ways we develop to inhibit discharge itself. In addition, Chapter 5 shows that the chronic patterns include all of the effects of oppression on us. My observation is that by the time we are 5 years old, the people around us rarely have a relationship with our inherent human nature, looking and reaching for the best in us, but rather relate only to our chronic patterns and the habits we have developed to cope with the difficulties surrounding us.

IMPLICATIONS FOR THE ABILITY OF PEOPLE TO LEAD

The result of this process is that everyone comes to the workplace with some limitations placed on their ability to function. Our self-esteem, our sense of self-worth, and our ability to take ourselves seriously are all damaged, and our

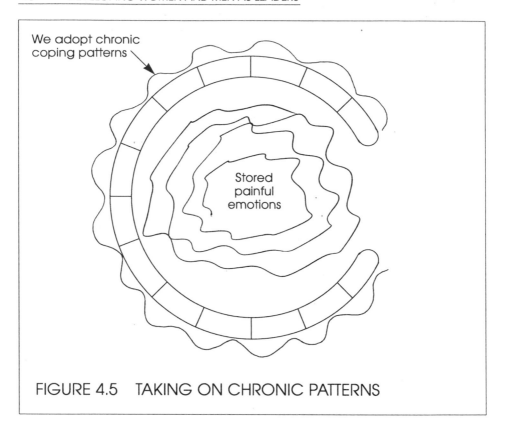

We adopt chronic coping patterns

Stored painful emotions

FIGURE 4.5   TAKING ON CHRONIC PATTERNS

response may have been to give up on ourselves in many small and large ways. Our ability to think flexibly, to use our capacity for making a fresh, new and appropriate response to each new situation is reduced, and our ability to be powerful in asserting our ideas and opinions is drastically reduced.

As a consequence, most people find it very difficult to function effectively as leaders. Our ability to fully understand the whole situation and to decide to see to it that everything in it goes well can be badly affected by the ways in which we have been hurt. The situation is then exacerbated by the culture of traditional leadership which emphasizes 'Do it on your own', 'Don't ever ask for help', 'You are better than everyone else', and 'Compete, win and get on with the task'.

Those of us who appear able to handle our turbulent environment successfully are, of course, just as hurt as anyone else, but perhaps have chronic patterns that 'fit' the expressed needs of the organization for a particular type of behaviour. For example, we may well be driven by the desire to prove that we are good enough and are therefore prepared to ride rough-shod over other people regardless of the real needs of the situation or whether we hurt anybody. Indeed, it is often people who have been hurt in these particular ways who then re-create the traditional leadership culture.

However, it *is* possible to recover from this situation if certain conditions are present.

PEOPLE CAN RECOVER FROM THE EFFECTS OF PAST HURTS

People can improve. This is a crucial viewpoint and it is the logical conclusion of the assumptions proposed above. While the hurts we receive do place limits on our ability to function, we can also assume that the inherent nature of people is still intact and that we retain the possibility of reclaiming our full, flexible intelligence, no matter how hurt we have been in the past.

If we take this viewpoint, we are in a position to make the very exciting proposal that improved functioning and even recovery is possible, but under one condition – that there is a sufficient 'contradiction' present in the workplace to the negative feelings that we may have about ourselves.

I define a contradiction as any intervention or positive direction coming from outside a person that provides the opportunity for that person to perceive the negative feelings about her- or himself or her or his situation, as not reality in the present. For example, where a person is being reminded of a previous hurtful situation and feels as though it is happening now, it is a very helpful contradiction to remind the person that this is a completely different situation and hence she or he is free to decide how to act in it now.

For example, for people who sometimes feel depressed and hopeless about life, a wonderful mountain view or an exquisite piece of music can be an important contradiction to their typical view of the world. For people who feel isolated and alone a cuddle with their dog or a hug from a friend is enough. Certainly, success is always a contradiction – look at what happens when people are very successful in sport, illustrated by the mixture of wild joy and profuse crying of the young cox in Britain's rowing team after winning the gold medal in the 1992 Olympic Games.

Having 'sufficient' contradiction means that, relative to the 'size' of the hurt that we carry around with us, there is a large enough intervention that it actually forces us to distinguish between the past and the present. Consequently, we have often accurately perceived what other people need to do to give them a hand, but we just don't do enough of it to make a real difference.

WHAT IS A CONTRADICTION?

A 'contradiction' is anything that allows the bearer of a pattern to perceive the pattern as not present-time reality.

It includes:
- giving the person your complete attention;
- showing them that you like them;
- getting them to do self-appreciation;
- appreciating them specifically and unconditionally.

FIGURE 4.6   WHAT IS A CONTRADICTION?

In the chapters which follow I shall introduce a variety of different contradictions as positive directions for taking our leadership forward as men and women.

REFERENCES

1.   *The Human Side of Human Beings*, Harvey Jackins (Rational Island Press, 1971).

5

HOW OPPRESSION DAMAGES
LEADERSHIP POTENTIAL

❖

In this chapter, I examine the effects that living in a society like ours has on people's leadership. I shall propose that people are not only hurt as individuals, but also damaged by the effects of institutionalized discrimination and prejudice directed at them because of their membership of particular groups. I show that such discrimination is rooted in a wider system of 'oppression', analyse its causes and describe how it works. I explore the way in which people 'internalize' the oppression and the effects of this on their leadership. I describe the different kinds of oppression that exist and their function in the system as a whole. Finally, I consider the effects of this process on the ability of people to lead.

In working with people in the context of their membership of particular groups, I have developed a number of perspectives about how society and organizations hurt people. They are the following:

1. People are hurt as an integral part of a wider system of institutionalized discrimination.

2. Institutionalized discrimination in organizations is rooted in a wider system that we could call the 'oppressive society'.

3. The oppressive society is maintained primarily by a 'cycle of oppression'.

4. The 'mechanism of oppression' makes it likely that members of an oppressed group will move into the role of oppressor towards others.

5. There are many different kinds of oppression in our organizations and society.

6. Oppression becomes institutionalized into discriminatory practices in organizations that deny access, training and promotion to the members of certain groups.

7. This process makes it more difficult for people to see themselves as potential leaders and damages their ability to lead.

49

PERSPECTIVE 1

People are hurt as an integral part of a wider system of institutionalized discrimination.

People are hurt not only by accident or by the process of 'contagion', but also by the existence of a system of institutionalized discrimination that has grown up towards people in particular groups, where prejudice and negative stereotyping is used as an excuse for the discrimination.

Thus, discrimination, for example against women in certain occupations, is based on a 'socially accepted' view about women which holds that they are inherently less able than men or less able at certain things (or more able in jobs that are 'boring and repetitive', but not in 'more demanding' jobs) and that it is therefore 'acceptable' to discriminate against them. This underlying anti-female conditioning is then institutionalized in personnel and employment policies that support the prejudice and are supported by it in turn.

PERSPECTIVE 2

Institutionalized discrimination in organizations is rooted in a wider system that we could call the 'oppressive society'.

If we look more deeply we can see that we are examining something much larger than institutionalized discrimination within organizations. We are examining, in fact, a wider social process that we could call 'oppression', which I define as:

> *The one-way, systematic and institutionalized mistreatment of one group of people, either by another group acting as the agents of society as a whole or by society as a whole.*

This implies that oppression is targeted in one direction only, towards the group being mistreated. As a consequence, members of the oppressed group usually suffer all or some of a number of disadvantages such as earning less, having less access to institutions, jobs, promotion or training, seeing fewer people like themselves in the predominant positions of power or having worse working and living conditions. They also often face a greater risk of ill-health, abuse and violence. I call these the 'objective conditions of oppression'; they can be measured, it is possible to demonstrate that they exist, and organizations such as the Equal Opportunities Commission or the Commission for Racial Equality often do so.

The definition also assumes that oppression is part of a wider system in which we all participate, and on whose behalf we act and maintain certain ways of behaving, rather than the traditional view that there is a 'conspiracy' by a particular group who have a vested interest in maintaining the status quo.

There are certain conditions where members of one group act as the 'agents' of oppression on behalf of society as a whole. Descriptions of this situation are now in common use and well understood. For example, we talk of 'racism' as the institutionalized mistreatment of black people by white people; of 'sexism' as the institutionalized mistreatment of women by men; and, in some circles of 'able-bodiedism' as the institutionalized mistreatment of people with disabilities. However, examples of oppression where there is no group in the targeting role but where the oppression comes from the society as a whole are less well known or understood. However, three stand out: the oppression of single people, parents and men.

In the case of single people, there is a clear economic mistreatment in the way products and services are still 'packaged' for families even though fewer than half the adult population now lives in the traditional nuclear family. However, there are also powerful negative prejudices in many cultures towards single people, such as the pressure to find a partner because being single is not 'whole'. This is dramatized particularly at women in the notion of an unmarried woman being an 'old maid' or 'spinster'.

In the case of parents, it is clear that at the point at which people need more resources to support a new family, they are expected to make do with less. Generally one parent generally has to leave work to undertake childcare or both parents have to pay a third person to do it, who is usually a woman on low wages. Moreover, there is an attitude in most cultures that children are seen as being the responsibility solely of their biological parents rather than everyone's future. Furthermore, among parents, single parents are often some of the poorest people in our society, and the great majority of single parents are female.

In the case of men, there is an underlying expectation that they will act as 'warriors' or 'breadwinners' and support the oppression of women, regardless of their specific personal needs at the human level, and they are systematically mistreated as young people in order to prepare them for that role.

In each of these cases the mistreatment can be called oppression because it is one-way, systematic and institutionalized, although there is no identified group of oppressors who are targeting the oppressed group; rather, the mistreatment comes from society as a whole. Later in this chapter, I shall describe these oppressions in more detail and I deal with men in particular in Chapters 8 and 9.

WHAT PURPOSE DOES OPPRESSION SERVE?

I have often been asked what purpose this system of oppression serves. Of course, it has no rational, pro-human purpose, but as far as I can tell, its main effect is to create and maintain apparent divisions of interest between human beings and thereby perpetuate an irrational world economic system that exploits the great majority of us and steals the inherent humanness of us all.

In saying this, I assume, as I said in Chapter 1, that we long ago reached the point where we actually have enough resources, wealth, technology and information to guarantee everyone a good life. However, since life on the planet for the very great majority is marked by insecurity, poverty and the constant fear of violence, while a minority live with more wealth than they can possibly spend, I think it is fair to describe our present economic system as an irrational one. Certainly, it is not working effectively for most people. Ironically, we find ourselves in a situation where four-fifths of the world is hungry while the remaining 20 per cent are dieting.

Once in place, oppression always uses some aspect of the appearance or behaviour of the group concerned as the excuse or justification for the mistreatment. The excuses mask the real reason, and these stereotypes are employed commonly and constantly to justify the mistreatment. The result is that we are divided and set against one another, making cooperation and agreement between us difficult, if not impossible.

PERSPECTIVE 3

The oppressive society is maintained primarily by a 'cycle of oppression'.

In earlier times, and in many parts of the world still, oppressive systems have been kept intact by the use of force and intimidation. In our society oppression has become more complex; essentially, each of us is conditioned into taking on the roles of both oppressed and oppressor, so that we end up oppressing one another. This is achieved primarily by conditioning people first to accept that the prejudice is true about them, and second, to agree to the mistreatment as though it were justified. I will call this process 'internalizing' the oppression.

The process is shown diagrammatically in Figure 5.1. Element (1) defines oppression. Elements (2) and (3) state that oppression comprises, on the one hand, the 'objective conditions' of the oppression – all the ways in which members of a group are discriminated against in terms of equality of access, promotion, and so on – and on the other hand, the 'subjective conditions' – the prejudice and negative stereotypes held about the members of the group and used to justify their mistreatment. For example, people are stereotyped and portrayed as 'stupid', 'not worth very much' or, in some way, 'uncontrollable'.

Both the objective and the subjective conditions of oppression are built on a web of misinformation and incorrect assumptions. It is an inherent part of our human nature that everyone, without exception, resists to whatever extent they can, given the resources they have around them (element 4). Under conditions of pressure, however, people may begin to 'agree' that they and others in their group are the way that the stereotypes describe them and they may even 'accept' that the oppression is justified.

I call this 'internalized oppression' and it is shown in element (5). It can be summarized in a number of statements that describe how people feel about themselves and their own group, how they mistreat themselves and other members of their own group, and how they allow other people to mistreat them and mistreat other members of their own group. I have laid this out in detail below.

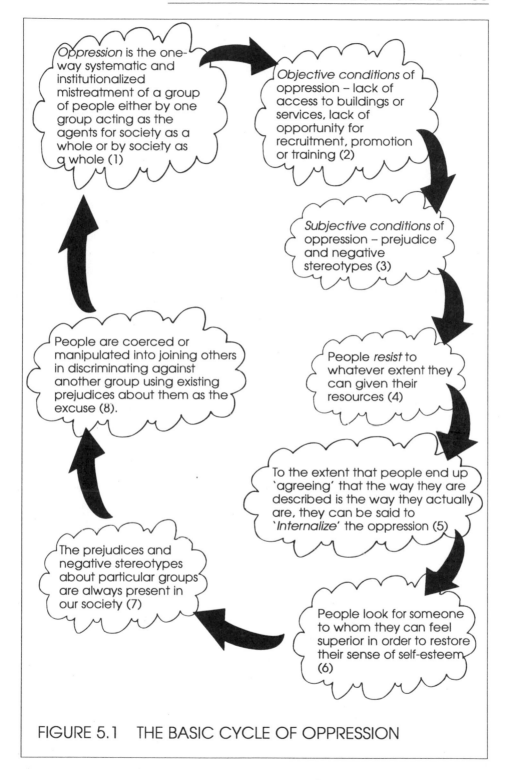

FIGURE 5.1   THE BASIC CYCLE OF OPPRESSION

Internalized oppression comprises the following:

○   All of the ways people feel badly about themselves as members of their own group.
○   All of the ways people feel badly about other members of their own group.
○   All of the ways people mistreat themselves.
○   All of the ways people mistreat other members of their own group.
○   All the ways people agree to allow other people to mistreat them as members of their own group.
○   All the ways people agree to allow other people to mistreat other members of their own group.

Once members of a group have internalized the prejudice and negative stereotypes about themselves, the internalization is sufficient to maintain the status quo. This explains, for example, why many women do not look for any kind of advancement beyond basic employment, saying, perhaps, 'I'm not good enough for anything better, and besides, I don't want the extra responsibility'. Thus, sexism conditions women to settle for less in their lives than they are really capable of and they then become antagonistic to proposals that they deserve better or should aim for more.

The concept of 'internalized oppression' is important if we are to understand why people first become 'their own worst enemy' and then become the oppressors of others.

Exercise 5.1   Understanding the effect that internalized oppression has upon us

Take a sheet of paper and divide it in three. In the left-hand column make a list of all the ways that you behave in each of the ways described above, as a woman or as a man. Then, in the middle column, write down against each mistreatment your best guess as to why you agreed to behave that way. Finally, in the third column, write down what feelings you would have to face if you were to stop behaving that way.

PERSPECTIVE 4

The 'basic mechanism of oppression' makes it likely that members of an oppressed group will move into the role of oppressor towards others.

To the extent that people accept the mistreatment, they look for ways of restoring their sense of their own value and self-esteem and risk taking on an attitude of 'superiority' towards some other group (element 6). This can make them prey to the variety of prejudices and negative stereotypes that exist about many other groups (element 7).

When people move into the role of oppressor towards another group, I call this 'the basic mechanism of oppression'. People are invited or manipulated into taking on the oppressor role towards another group and feel 'justified' in their mistreatment of them because of the negative stereotypes that exist. This is shown in element (8) and means that the cycle of oppression is complete – effectively, the oppressed becomes the oppressor. It is particularly common where people already feel hard done by in terms of policies, space or perhaps money – it is easy to rouse people's bad feelings towards another group rather than towards the real cause, namely, the way the system is set up as a whole.

Most of us are completely unaware that this process is taking place because we are conditioned to believe that 'this is just the way the world is' – we are, after all, only being treated in the same way that everyone has always been treated. Generation after generation, we have been made to feel bad about ourselves as members of a particular group, for example males, and then, in the absence of a hand to help us understand the truth about our inherent nature or deal with how painful our own mistreatment is, we are invited to mistreat the members of another group – females – in the desperate hope that we will feel better about ourselves. It is as though everyone is given a stick that is both long enough and short enough to beat everyone including oneself. We are all both oppressor and oppressed.

The effect of this is to divide people, to make it difficult for people to reach for cooperation and win–win, and to divert their attention away from what is really going on towards personal concerns.

PERSPECTIVE 5

There are many different kinds of oppression in our organizations and society.

In growing up and living in a society like ours, everyone is likely to be oppressed in several different ways Each oppression serves a specific purpose and contributes in a particular way to the overall divisions that exist between people.

Unfortunately, people working towards the elimination of a particular oppression are often pitted against others who are working towards the elimination of another oppression. They might claim 'The way I have been oppressed is worse than the way you have been oppressed', as though there were some competition about who has suffered the worst.

In fact, all oppressions are equally important, because the perpetuation of every single oppression is crucial to the maintenance of all oppressions. If we remember that the basic purpose of all oppression is to divide us, we can see that advancing the position that 'my oppression is worse than yours' is actually divisive. This kind of competition, which is another form of 'internalized oppression', usually takes place either because the oppression of a particular group is not being addressed sufficiently or because the members of the group are frightened that this is the case.

It follows that to eliminate any oppression we need to stand four square against the oppression of every other group and build effective alliances with their members in order to break down the imposed divisions within and across all groups. To achieve this we must understand the purpose and content of each oppression. Let us look at a number of different oppressions and the purpose that they seem to serve. I will begin with the oppression of young people, and then examine classism, national oppressions, sexism, heterosexism, racism, anti-Jewish oppression, able-bodiedism, ageism, and mental health oppression.

EXAMPLES OF OPPRESSION

The word *adultism* has been used to describe the oppression of young people. It is the first oppression we experience and, since we have all been young people, we will all have suffered from it. It is rooted in the assumption that a person is not a full human being with full human rights until a certain age is reached. Probably the best example of it in our culture is the old Victorian notion that 'Children should be seen and not heard!'. It seems designed to prepare us for our future role as the agents of oppression by dividing us and setting us against one another at an early age through the installation of the basic mechanism of oppression.

It does this first by encouraging adults to treat young people with less than complete respect; young people often 'internalize' this as a sense of powerlessness and low self-esteem. They are then invited to mistreat the members of other groups of young people who may be different from themselves in some way.

In organizations, adultism takes the form of regarding young workers as having little to contribute because of their youth and inexperience. It continues in a less extreme but still significant form towards young adults up to and including people in their late 20s.

Classism is the oppression of all people who work for wages. This, of course, is most of the population. It robs people of their sense of their real human worth and replaces it with an evaluation of their value based upon how much they get paid, how high in the hierarchy they sit, how big their desk is, how big a house they have or how expensive their car is. In reality, we can never measure the value of a human being on the basis of money or possessions; human beings are priceless. Classism, however, communicates that people who work for wages, particularly if they work with their hands, are generally not bright enough to take charge of their own lives.

During the past 50 years there has been an attempt to demonstrate that oppression based on class no longer exists and certainly the lives of many people in the developed world have advanced to an extraordinary extent. However, the underlying attitudes and mistreatment have not been eliminated and the distribution of wealth and income as between the richest and poorest has widened considerably during the past 15 years. Moreover, the fundamental issue is ownership and the control that it brings; despite many attempts to widen share purchase, ownership and real control still rests in the hands of a small group of people.

Classism is built into the very foundations of the contemporary organization and is a fundamental cause of its ineffectiveness. This has not been better dramatized than in the quotation from Makushita that I reported in Chapter 2:

> For you the essence of management is getting the ideas out of the heads of management into the hands of labour. For us, the art of management is mobilizing and pulling together the intellectual resources of all the employees in the service of the firm ... Only by drawing on the combined brainpower of all its employees can a firm face up to the turbulence and constraints of today's environment.

Classist attitudes and behaviour are rife in organizational life. Indeed, the very structure of the organization as a hierarchy, if the people in formal leadership positions think that they are more important than others, is intrinsically classist. The traditional assumption, described in Chapter 2, that managers are inherently more intelligent and able than the people they lead, has the effect of separating them and making them feel superior. The assumption on the part of non-managers that they are not cut out for leadership, or that they are less intelligent and less able, is equally rooted in classism.

Nationalism has re-emerged as being significant during the past ten years all over the world. In the pursuit of economic survival, there has been a resurgence of interest in national identity and the defence of the nation-state. This becomes a *national oppression* when it leads the members of a nation to act to dominate another nation using aspects of the behaviour of members of that nation as the excuse.

The war in what used to be Yugoslavia, the continuing conflicts within the old Soviet Union and the aggression against Tibet by China, are all examples of national oppression at work.

Sexism is the oppression of women by men acting as the agents of society as a whole. Its purpose seems to be to make it very difficult for women and men to work together effectively.

The effect of sexism within organizations is that men are still the predominant group in formal leadership positions, even though women are entering the workforce in increasing numbers in junior positions, often involving part-time work.

The oppression of women will be dealt with in more detail in Chapters 6 and 7.

Heterosexism is the oppression of gay men, lesbians and bisexual people. Its purpose is to leave all people frightened of building close, warm and dependable relationships with people of the same sex for fear of being targeted by gay oppression. It has the effect of dividing man from man and woman from woman.

In an organization, heterosexism plays a key role in establishing a culture of aloofness and distance, especially between people of the same sex. I have noticed that men in organizations in particular keep considerable distance between one another, rarely expressing appreciation or warmth, for fear of being thought gay. This is often called 'homophobia', the fear of closeness between people of the same sex.

Racism is the oppression of a group on the basis of their nationality or culture. In our society it is aimed at black people, the Irish, Jews and others. Racism demeans all cultures by suggesting that there is an 'ordinary' or 'normal' way to be. The purpose it appears to serve is to cause all of us to be frightened of differences and determined to be as much as possible the 'same' as those with power.

Racism towards black people is the oppression of the members of a group using colour as the excuse for that mistreatment. The logical progression from this is that white people and their culture are superior and that black people are inferior. Again, the purpose of racism is that it seems to encourage the pursuit of the 'normal' and the fear of difference.

Anti-Jewish oppression (or as it is sometimes known, though incorrectly, 'anti-Semitism') is the oppression of Jews. After the Exodus from Israel, Jews were invited into many countries and then used in particular roles such as money lenders, only to be 'scapegoated' later, as in Nazi Germany, when they were no longer needed in that role. This has the effect of being an 'opening wedge' that permits subsequent attacks on other groups. The effect of this oppression upon Jewish people is to instil a chronic fear of being attacked that tends to lead them to prefer isolation in the hope of remaining safe.

Able-bodiedism is the oppression of people with disabilities (which includes many more of us than we usually admit). In a society which prizes most highly the ability to work and produce, people with disabilities are seen as less important because they are considered non-productive. This makes us all fearful of becoming disabled ourselves and therefore serves to keep us working hard even when we need a break. The content of the oppression is the communication to disabled people that they are not valuable.

In an organization, the effect of this is to make it less likely that people will speak up when they are not well, more likely to hide any disability they might have if at all possible, and often relegated to a junior position if they are actually disabled.

Since we all tend to develop disabilities as we grow older, the oppression of disabled people links to *ageism* which is the oppression of older people. In our culture, older people are often regarded as less able and sometimes even a nuisance, rather than as people with great wisdom and many skills to offer. This is a further reinforcement of the practice of 'valuing' people only as producers and devaluing them as human beings. It leaves us all frightened of ageing and leaves older people and the people caring for them very isolated.

Mental health oppression is the oppression of people who have difficulty in conforming to so-called 'normal' ways of behaving. Some people can be hurt so badly that their ability to function within the 'limits' of what is regarded as 'normal' is severely damaged. They may then be treated as though they are less than fully human, rather than as human beings with certain learning difficulties. Mental health oppression is a key component in the structure of the oppressive society in that the purpose it serves is to keep all other oppressions in place in a very direct way by making everyone frightened of showing their emotions.

However, any kind of mistreatment hurts a great deal and the natural response, as described in Chapter 4, is to call attention to the hurt, seek to discharge, and then to resist the mistreatment. Mental health oppression seeks to deny or decry this process, meaning that everyone is made fearful of the essential recovery and healing process because it appears to signal being disturbed and out of control. In some situations (for example, extensively in the old Soviet Union) people who resist oppression have been 'imprisoned' in hospitals for the so-called mentally ill and treated with electro-shock therapy or drugs in order to 'cure' them.

In organizations, mental health oppression has the effect of making everyone frightened of admitting that they don't know how to do things or of getting upset about how they are being treated. It is a particularly important issue in relationships between women and men because the gender conditioning of women tends to leave them with the discharge process more intact than men, and as a consequence men can become hostile if women get 'upset' at work.

OPPRESSION WHERE THERE IS NO GROUP TARGETING ANOTHER GROUP

Most oppressions cast the members of other groups as the agents of the oppression on behalf of society as a whole, as, for example, whites in the case of racism towards black people. However, there are a number of oppressions that do not have a particular group acting as the agents but rather the oppression is carried out by society as a whole. The three described earlier in this chapter were the oppression of single people, of parents, and of men.

The oppression of *single people* is that of people who have chosen or found themselves following a 'single' life-style. The suggestion is that it is 'normal' for people to be married, and probably to have children. Society is still largely structured to support the traditional nuclear family, and life styles that differ tend to be frowned on. Food, holidays and housing are often 'packaged' for the nuclear family.

It is closely connected to gay oppression, because gay men and lesbians will often 'hide' their life-style and as a consequence be asked 'When are you going to settle down with a nice boy/girl?'.

The oppression of *parents* exploits the work of childcare workers. Because young people are not productive workers, they are not highly valued and therefore caring for them is not highly valued. Consequently, the work of childcare is done free or on the cheap. This tends to perpetuate adultism by putting parents into situations where they are undersupported and often exhausted.

With large numbers of women entering the workforce, this is of great importance. Female parents are still expected to combine their parenting with work, while many male parents continue to concentrate on work. Thus women are often sceptical about the possibility of handling two demanding roles, and they may well hold back from reaching for formal leadership positions. A fundamental improvement in our understanding about the importance of parenting is necessary if we are to enable both women and men to contribute fully to our organizations and to leadership in them.

Men are oppressed as a group by society, but not by women or children. The purpose of the oppression of men is to encourage them to be warriors, to see themselves primarily as breadwinners and wage earners, producing more than they need just to support themselves, and to become the agents of the oppression of women. The brutalization of men robs them of their connection to their humanness and reduces the possibility of building nurturing and caring relationships with other men and with women. I deal with the oppression of men in more detail in Chapters 8 and 9.

PERSPECTIVE 6

Oppression becomes institutionalized into discriminatory practices in organizations that deny access, training and promotion to the members of certain groups.

Of course, people bring their behaviour and prejudices to work; indeed, the workplace provides a major learning environment about oppression. Over time, the cycle of oppression can become institutionalized into the common practices and procedures of the organization so as to deny the members of particular groups access, training and promotion. This process is then defended as the way it should be since it has always been that way.

Institutionalized discrimination can be both direct or indirect. Direct discrimination consists of treating a person less favourably than others in the same or similar circumstance. Indirect discrimination consists of applying in any circumstances a requirement or condition which, although applied equally to persons of other groups, is such that only a considerably smaller proportion of the targeted group can comply with it and where this cannot be shown to be justifiable on grounds other than discrimination.

PERSPECTIVE 7

This process makes it more difficult for people to see themselves as potential leaders and damages their ability to lead.

I have argued throughout this book that leadership is a natural attribute of our inherent nature. Oppression creates a situation where some people are offered opportunities to lead while others are denied them because of their membership of particular groups. Thus mistreatment is reinforced and justified by prejudice and stereotypes about both groups.

In reality, both oppressors and oppressed are hurt by this process. Oppressors are hurt because they have to take on an inhuman view of the ability and value of other people. It is very hard to put people at the heart of everything we do if we believe that we are superior and others are inferior.

Members of the oppressed group are hurt because people internalize the oppression and this internalized oppression has a limiting effect on their ability to function. It is a key hurt that leads people to have less confidence, to accept the status quo and to settle for less. People are less ambitious, have fewer opportunities to practise and improve, and ultimately 'prove that what is said about them is true'. This is certainly true in the case of women.

6

THE UNDERMINING OF WOMEN'S LEADERSHIP

❖

In my work with women and men over many years, I have had the opportunity to work with a number of very thoughtful and powerful women colleagues and I have listened to many hundreds of women speaking to men about their experience of working in organizations and developing their leadership. The experience of working with and listening to these women has had a profound effect on my attitudes and on my understanding of the situation that women face. In particular I have drawn heavily on and am indebted to the work of Rosemary Brennan.[1]

In this chapter I explore what it would mean to put women at the centre. I assess the present situation facing women based on my studies and my experience of listening to women talk about themselves, examine how women 'internalize' sexism and gender conditioning and look at the effects of all this on their opportunity and ability to lead. I begin, however, by outlining what it might be like when women are at the heart of our organizations.

PUTTING WOMEN AT THE CENTRE

Imagine what an organization will be like when women are included at every level and in every occupation. Of course, there would not be exactly equal numbers of women and men anywhere, but women would be present in the board room alongside the men as chief executives, as non-executive directors, as production managers, as marketing specialists, as the finance director, as the executive responsible for human resources. There would be plenty of women engineers, software experts, refuse collectors, bus drivers and footballers. Whenever a big decision was being made, women would be making a key contribution, listened to and respected and bringing a different perspective to the problem because of their experience. Women would be central to the organization at every level and in every function.

In order to build our organizations that way, we need to understand how women are excluded and what happens to inhibit them from taking their rightful place. We must develop strategies to ensure that they are present at every level, in every occupation and in the forefront of leadership.

THE PRESENT SITUATION

Eliminating sexism is a battle half won. The understanding that sexism is unacceptable both at the interpersonal and the institutional level has grown enormously during the past two decades. Much of this has been due to the success of the women's movement across the developed world in forcing people to discuss and accept that women have faced a systematic discrimination and that we must work to create a culture in which women can expect to be fully included and have equality of opportunity. There is hardly an area of public or private life that has not come under close scrutiny by women and their allies and great battles have been fought and won. Let us look at a few areas.

ARE WOMEN AND MEN DIFFERENT?

The debate over whether there are inherent differences between women and men continues, but there is now general agreement that there are more commonalities than differences. It is increasingly understood that there are greater differences for any given attribute within each group than between the groups. So, in terms of physical capacity for example, the range of heights, weights or strengths from the lowest to the highest vary more among women than they do between women or men.

Similarly, in terms of ability to function intellectually, the spread of ability is wider among women than it is between the two sexes. It is certainly true that, as intelligence and psychological testing have been improved, women have been shown to perform as well as men (though whether such tests actually offer any useful information about a person's ability is still a moot point).

There is no difference in the ability of women and men to work hard. Research by the United Nations has shown that in the world as a whole, women comprise 51 per cent of the population, do 66 per cent of the work, receive 10 per cent of the income, and own less than 1 per cent of the property.

Most people would now agree that other apparent differences in the ability of women and men to function effectively are a product of the effects of oppression. Sexism has two effects: on the one hand, through institutional discrimination, it reduces women's actual opportunities and, on the other, through 'internalized oppression', it leads women to accept barriers which some are able to overcome but which many do not. In the case of men, what I will call 'men's oppression' in later chapters tends to limit men to valuing a focus on the task and personal achievement rather than working closely and cooperatively with other people.

THE LEGISLATION

In much of the developed world there is now legislation to protect women against discrimination and in some countries affirmative action policies have been developed to ensure that women advance to their rightful position alongside men. In the United Kingdom, for example, there has been legislation since 1975 aimed at protecting women and men alike from inequality of opportunity in the workplace and a body of case law stemming from this has made some impact on reducing the willingness of people in organizations to discriminate against women.

However, in many situations where cases of discrimination have seemed justified, and therefore winnable, tribunals have not ruled in favour of the woman and this legislation is now generally regarded as not working very effectively. In recent years, greater successes have been achieved under European legislation in cases taken to the European Court of Human Rights.

There is a continuing debate about the fairness of positive discrimination as a tool for advancing women into leadership, but most people accept the importance of developing positive action strategies which aim to give women a fair chance when the opportunity arises. However, we need to continue to review and improve the legislation covering equality of opportunity if we are to make real progress in advancing women's position.

ENTRY INTO THE WORKFORCE

Women have been entering many occupations in greater numbers and this is gradually leading to a transformation in the complexion of the workforce, with almost as many women now working as men. Historically, however, women have been excluded from most organizations. In the United Kingdom, for example, women made up 35.5 per cent of the total workforce in 1960 and only in the last ten years has the number of women at work increased to some 49.5 per cent. Many of these jobs are junior positions with lower wages and worse working conditions than male colleagues and many of them are ghetto-ized into particular fields. Thirty per cent of them are part-time. The total number of women on the boards of major British companies is 3.72 per cent, while women make up only 2.8 per cent of senior managers and 9.8 per cent of managers as a whole.

The number of traditional full-time jobs for men in the UK has collapsed over the last 15 years by two million, and between 1960 and 1990 the number of working women rose by 34 per cent while the number of working men fell 20 per cent. As a consequence, women are increasingly in direct competition with men for work. However, many jobs still remain behind a door that is more or less shut to women.

Overall, women's wages continue to lag behind those of men and in many countries in the developed world the gap is either static or has even been increasing since 1980. Women are located in their greatest numbers in occupations such as nursing, teaching, childcare, social work and administration, and these are consistently underfunded compared with other jobs. The economic exploitation of women's work continues to be a major cause of their difficulties in taking on full leadership in our society.

The average female worker earns nearly 40 per cent less than the average male earner and women managers earn 16 per cent less than their male counterparts. Young women have personal incomes 14 per cent higher than the female average. Women have received much less training than men and their chances of promotion have been systematically curtailed. They have often been patronized, ignored and harassed. Women's experience of life in organizations has not been a good one.

Some progress has been achieved, but we are still only half way. If we are to win the battle for complete equality of opportunity for women and then move ahead to build an inclusive organization, it is essential to create the conditions in which women will want to lead and will feel supported as they do so. These conditions need to include pay equality as well as equality of opportunity at all levels.

WOMEN AND LEADERSHIP

While the attitude of many women to taking on formal and informal leadership has changed dramatically and they are increasingly keen to join men in leading our organizations, many women still find themselves blocked. On the one hand, managers in many organizations still covertly operate old prejudices when selecting or appointing women and on the other hand, many women still limit their own aspirations because of lack of confidence or fear about their ability to lead.

The challenge is to scrutinize these external and internal blocks and then plan to eliminate them systematically. For the remainder of this chapter, my primary interest is in examining the blocks which women carry within themselves to taking full leadership in every situation and then making proposals as to how women and men can work cooperatively to overcome the blocks.

THE INTERNAL BLOCKS TO WOMEN'S LEADERSHIP

In Chapters 4 and 5, I showed that people are not born with the patterns of oppressor or oppressed but that these roles and behaviours are the product of a system of oppression. I demonstrated that oppression comprises both the objective conditions of institutionalized discrimination and the subjective conditions of negative stereotypes and prejudices that are used to justify the discrimination.

In organizations, it operates to exclude women from the centre of events and has a profound effect on how they think and feel about themselves and their leadership. This oppression is called sexism and we can define it as the *one way, systematic and institutionalized mistreatment of women by men using prejudices and negative stereotypes about women as the excuse for the mistreatment*. As a result, women are likely to 'internalize' the messages of institutional discrimination and prejudice, ending up believing that the messages are true about themselves.

Women in general, and young women in particular, seem to have made great progress in combating this process. They are more confident, less prepared to tolerate mistreatment and work more effectively together than ever before. Nevertheless, the process still goes on and women do take on and believe that the prejudices and negative stereotypes are true.

Why do women internalize sexism? It is a consequence of being subjected to the process of 'gender conditioning.' It begins with little girls and young women and is designed to prepare them for their future role in life and to secure their agreement to live within the limits of that prescribed role. In order to achieve this it is necessary to 'invent' a set of culturally acceptable characteristics that describe a 'real woman', which are then applied to each woman in order to demonstrate that she is only acceptable if she behaves within the limits of these characteristics. They change over time and are different in different groups depending on race, class or perhaps nationality.

Work in the area of gender studies during the past 20 years has identified many of these 'culturally acceptable' characteristics but for the purposes of this chapter

---

Exercise 6.1   Female stereotypes

Take a sheet of paper and pen and write down all the stereotype behaviour you were brought up to expect from 'real women'. Here is a start – 'Real women' are kind, considerate, understanding, pretty, unambitious, ...'
Then write down how you feel when women do not behave according to the stereotype.

I have chosen six that the women I have worked with regard as particularly important in undermining women's leadership. They are:

○   'Real women' are sensitive and soft.
○   'Real women' care for other people.
○   'Real women' are expected to be slim, beautiful and well-dressed.
○   'Real women' experience the world as a frightening place.
○   'Real women' need a man to protect them.
○   'Real women' aren't leaders.

'REAL WOMEN' ARE SENSITIVE AND SOFT

In the white, North European culture that I have grown up in, little girls tend to be brought up to understand that, while it is true that feelings in general should be kept to oneself, certain kinds of feeling are acceptable and others are completely unacceptable.

There is an expectation that little girls will be more 'emotional' than little boys, although, of course, not too emotional. For example, it is more acceptable for girls to be sensitive, soft and to cry when they are hurting. They are expected to be frightened if there is aggression about and to not stand up for themselves. This aspect of gender conditioning is rooted in the belief that women's future role is still expected to be that of primary childcarer.

Later in life, women find that 'being too emotional' is itself a part of a negative stereotype about how women behave at work – if one gets 'too emotional', this leads to poor judgement on their part as well as being difficult for everyone else (particularly for men, as we will see in subsequent chapters).

Nevertheless, little girls are brought up with some expectation that being soft is acceptable and valued. However, expressing other feelings is quite unacceptable – for example, expressions of outrage and anger are considered 'unfeminine'. 'Real women' do not become hostile or demanding, turn violent, or make trouble.

This can create particular difficulties for women where their class position or culture encourages them to be powerful. For example, many Irish or Afro-Caribbean women play a stronger role in their families than do their men, perhaps deciding what will happen, holding the family together and solving particular difficulties. Similarly, some women with an upper-class background may obtain significant positions in the world of work or politics because of their confidence and powerful presentation. These situations can place special pressure on such women if the wider society says they 'should be' submissive.

'REAL WOMEN' CARE FOR OTHER PEOPLE

Women tend to be brought up not only to believe that being sensitive and soft is acceptable while being assertive or angry is not, but also to think that their 'role' in life is to put that sensitivity into actively caring for others. Of course, caring is an inherent human characteristic and absolutely essential to the well-being of both givers and receivers. However, gender conditioning implies that it is primarily women who need to develop this ability, while if it were extensively developed in a man it would be thought of as 'unmanly'.

The underlying motivation for this conditioning is, apparently, once again to prepare women for motherhood. Therefore, little girls are appreciated and encouraged for any action which demonstrates caring, for example by being told that they are 'little angels'. Many women are still given tasks in the home and expected to fulfil them well from a very early age while their brothers are not asked or are given tasks that are identified as masculine. Indeed, some young women run the home if their mother is disabled or dies, though this is much less common among young men in a similar position.

This means that there is a heavy conditioning towards, and some specific training for, looking after other people's feelings, making people feel at ease, and helping people if they appear to be hurting in some way. It is reinforced through the purchase of dolls and other items of toy household equipment which little girls are expected to learn how to use.

Of course, this is played out in the workplace. People still expect women to make coffee and tea for their male bosses and peers. Women report that they are still asked in job interviews what their husbands will think about their being out at work (since clearly 'they should be at home looking after the house'). A young woman I know with a first class honours degree was asked in a recent interview for a public relations company about what her father did and what his interests and tastes were. Some married women are still asked whether they plan to have a baby, despite this being an illegal form of questioning, and is even addressed to highly successful women at the top of their profession. Much of the progress women have made into formal leadership positions in organizations has been in 'caring roles' such as personnel or public relations.

'REAL WOMEN' ARE EXPECTED TO BE SLIM, BEAUTIFUL AND WELL-DRESSED

There are very precisely defined characteristics that 'real women' are expected to aim for in their appearance. These characteristics change over time according to changes in fashions, but for much of the past 50 years women have been expected to meet criteria that emphasize slimness, beauty (as defined by Eurocentric definitions of beauty), and 'dress sense'. Very few women can meet these criteria, either because of their actual body structure or because of inadequate finances.

As a result, women look at and judge themselves through the eyes of others rather than through their own eyes, thus 'objectifying' themselves. Most women will experience a feeling of never being satisfied with the way they appear in the world, and, in circumstances where they must appear 'perfect', will have a very high level of stress if they are unable to achieve it.

This puts great pressure on women as leaders to make themselves look acceptable to a world that is primarily a man's world. The notion of 'power dressing' grew up in the 1980s among women who were trying to establish themselves in the workplace as somebody to be reckoned with. On the one hand, this often puts them into competition with other women for who looks the best in the eyes of others (usually men), and this can divide and make cooperation difficult. On the other hand, it has intimidated some men, who then begin to stereotype such women, as 'tough bitches'.

'REAL WOMEN' EXPERIENCE THE WORLD AS A FRIGHTENING PLACE

Women have always been brought up to see themselves as being 'at risk' in the world. Indeed, there has been a reported increase in violence towards women, particularly as the economic situation has worsened in recent years. I say 'reported' because the upturn in recorded events is real and there does appear to be an increase. However, it may well be that the actual number of incidents has not increased significantly but simply more are reported as the climate for reporting them improves.

Recently there have been some significant cases where sexual assault and harassment have been alleged, both in the United States and the United Kingdom, and these have created national and international discussion about what is appropriate behaviour between men and women in the workplace.

Throughout these events, the underlying message given to women time and again is 'You are not able to look after yourself and you need protection!'. This begins with little girls being told that they are unsafe in the world and then encouraged to see themselves as weak and dependent. Of course, there are very real reasons for taking care, but young women need guidance and training to be able to handle the situation rather than merely assuming weakness and dependency.

'REAL WOMEN' NEED A MAN TO PROTECT THEM

Sexism and heterosexism teach both women and men that they are incomplete without a member of the 'opposite sex' as a partner, and the man is intended to be the provider and protector while the woman is the carer. This is based on the negative stereotype just described, that women are the 'weaker sex' and are unable to look after themselves.

This injunction leads many women to accepting or pretending to accept a heavy dependency on men, regardless of the actual situation in terms of relative personal power or experience between any particular woman and man.

In the workplace, this leaves many women still stepping aside when a man, particularly if he is senior, starts to take over. In so many different situations there seems to be a tacit agreement between both parties that the man will lead – for example, whether on television or in real life, why is it always the male police officer who seems to drive the car?

'REAL WOMEN' AREN'T LEADERS

Women are seen as marginal to the world of affairs rather than central to them. The inevitable consequence of being conditioned to not put themselves first but to see their primary role as caring for others, is that women do not see themselves as appropriate leaders in a situation, where leadership is defined as 'working to understand the whole situation and deciding to see to it that absolutely everything in it goes well'. They are encouraged to fulfil their need for achievement through the achievement of others – for example clichés such as 'Women are the power behind the throne!', 'The hand that rocks the cradle rules the world!' or 'Behind every good man is a good woman' speak oceans on this situation.

This characterization is achieved in many different ways, much of it in the early years of life through the kind of games that women are encouraged or discouraged to play. Thus little girls are encouraged to 'play at' domestic tasks but discouraged from playing games with boys or from playing 'boys' games' because such games are considered 'rough' and therefore inappropriate. Girls who insist on playing such games are called 'tomboys' and teased about their behaviour as a further way of persuading them to stop. Later in life, women who behave in a powerful, assertive manner can be described as 'bossy' or 'pushy', or worse!

Traditionally, sexism has encouraged families to make their first priority providing sons with an education, while daughters have been encouraged to 'get a husband and settle down'. In recent years this practice has declined, but many parents still have a tendency to place more importance on their sons' education than their daughters'.

When exploring whether there are different educational abilities between males and females there is still one apparently well kept secret that throws much light on the question. When I discussed streaming with the headmaster of my children's school he told me that from age 12 upwards at secondary schools, girls should take almost all of the places in the top stream if performance was strictly taken into account. Apparently, schools maintain a quota of half girls and half boys in those streams, thus positively discriminating in favour of boys. Such quotas would be criticized unmercifully if they were proposed in order to advance women in organizations.

Once in the workplace, there are still many people in managerial and leadership positions with an underlying negative prejudice towards women being at work and moving into management, and they can block a woman's progress in many subtle and unsubtle ways. Moreover, when women look at the demands placed on managers in a 'traditional leadership' culture, many decide that this is something that they do not want and could not cope with given their other responsibilities. While more and more women have been able to ignore and escape this conditioning, it must undermine their aspirations to contribute and lead, and many agree to settle for more junior positions than their ability permits.

When we put the conditioning to be carers together with the conditioning not to take leadership, we have a situation that could be described as 'having responsibility without authority'. This places great stress on women, by pressuring them to try to make things 'right' for other people but having to do so in a 'caring' way rather than by taking charge. The resulting feelings of frustration and powerlessness must contribute to many of the so-called 'nervous breakdowns' that women experience and the predominance of women in mental institutions.

Figure 6.1 demonstrates the primary content of women's gender conditioning and its cumulative effect which appears to be that many women have lower expectations of themselves and their lives, preferring to accept less than to do battle for their just position.

SETTLING FOR LESS

Training to settle for less than absolutely everything for themselves, for their lives, for themselves as leaders, or for their world seems to be at the core of the gender conditioning that women receive. There are many examples of this in action. A significant example, historically, has been the way that women have often given more food to their partners and children rather than taking it for themselves, particularly where food is scarce. It is even surmised that this accounts for women's smaller average size than men's.

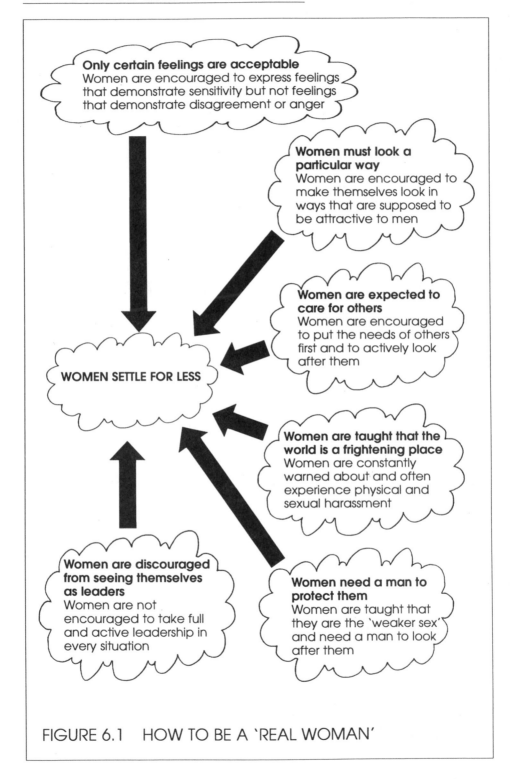

FIGURE 6.1   HOW TO BE A 'REAL WOMAN'

Settling for less is deeply rooted in the training to be a carer, to place the needs of others first, while at the same time not placing one's own needs centrally. Women find themselves still paying attention, listening and giving love when they are absolutely exhausted and ready to drop. They will frequently get up early in the morning before others rise in order to clean and wash the clothes.

In terms of leadership, women tend to be 'people orientated' rather than 'achievement orientated'. Judy Marshall writes, 'The most frequently reported difference [between women and men] is that women managers sometimes scored higher on the supporting dimensions of leadership than do male colleagues and showed a greater concern for relationships.'[2] In a new study that she undertook she found that women were considerably stronger than men in styles that emphasized teamwork, structuring the situation and consideration for others while men were more *laissez-faire* in their approach.

While in practice this is an extremely useful emphasis given the needs of the present situation, it can also discourage women from putting themselves forward for leadership. It has the effect of preventing women from thinking about their career because they are simply getting on with the job they have taken on. In the next chapter I shall examine what steps women need to take in order to challenge their internalized oppression and to take full leadership in the world and in their organizations.

REFERENCES

1. *Barriers to Women's Leadership*, Rosemary Brennan (Industrial and Commercial Training, 1987).
2. 'A Comparative Study of Gender and Management Style', Judi Marshall, (*Management Development Review*, Vol. 5, No. 1, 1992).

7

CHALLENGING WOMEN'S INTERNALIZED SEXISM

❖

Taking leadership – where we define leadership as working to understand the whole situation and deciding to see to it that absolutely everything in it goes well – is an integral part of everyone's inherent nature. Although it is often argued otherwise, it is not some special attribute allocated on the basis of class, gender, race or sex. Thus, every woman is born to lead.

The impact of gender conditioning and internalized sexism gives women some particular strengths and some real difficulties. The strengths lie in the particular experiences that women have to face but the difficulties are primarily a product of not taking one's self seriously, low self esteem and seeing oneself in competition with other women. The challenge is to help women use and develop their strengths and overcome their difficulties. This means bringing a number of different contradictions to bear in each of these areas.

THE STRENGTHS THAT WOMEN BRING TO LEADERSHIP

Any organization that does not have women in every occupation and at every level within it in roughly equal numbers to men is unlikely to be able to survive the crisis that we face. Women bring an insight, an understanding and skills to every situation that men are not able to offer because of the differences in conditioning.

To begin with, every group that experiences oppression and has some understanding of what it is experiencing, tends to have an empathy and compassion for others in the same position. Many women do have an understanding of how other people feel about their situation and what needs to be done about it that reaches beyond any understanding which most men are able to bring. Women are brought up to reach for and include other people where men are trained to look after themselves.

Moreover, because women are encouraged to care deeply for others and to put that care into practice in their relationships, they are able to do what needs

75

to be done with warmth and love. In this sense, we could say that women are trained to be 'other person centred' rather than 'self centred'. This is precisely the orientation that is needed to build an inclusive organization because it encourages leaders to put people at the heart of everything they do.

In putting their caring into practice, women are encouraged to listen rather than talk, to focus their attention on other people and the task in hand rather than trying to attract attention, and to show other people that they like and value them. These are crucial attributes in any new leadership initiative.

The encouragement not to see oneself as central means that women are keen to work together with others when undertaking tasks rather than seeking to 'glorify' their own position or contribution. While the low self-esteem which many women hold themselves in has to be challenged, it ensures that few women are arrogant or self-opinionated.

It also means that women are often able to see a much wider picture than the next step. The achievement and task-focus that many men have may get the job done, but it leads to a linear approach rather than a more holistic way of looking at things. Women tend to have more of a systems view, seeing the cause and effect and taking it into account in their leadership.

Women are also strong. Having to lead, while facing the effects of sexism and internalized sexism, ensures that women are hardy and determined in pursuit of their goals. They have known adversity and adversity is a great teacher.

There are many more exciting and important strengths that women are able to bring to bear. However, women's internalized oppression leaves them with very significant challenges which women and men need to work together to help women to overcome.

THE KEY CHALLENGES

There are many different challenges facing each woman, and each woman differs from others because each will have had a unique experience of life. However, the key challenges that women face will always be a function of the way in which each woman has internalized sexism. Chapter 5 described the most important characteristics of internalized oppression and when these are accepted by women as internalized sexism they become:

O   All of the ways that woman have ended up feeling badly about themselves.

O   All of the ways that women have ended up feeling badly towards other women.

O   All of the ways that women mistreat themselves.

O   All of the ways that women mistreat other women.

O   All of the ways that women allow themselves to be mistreated.

O   All of the ways that women allow other women to be mistreated.

Any programme aimed at developing women's leadership would need to offer a contradiction to each of these aspects of 'internalized sexism'.

CHALLENGING ALL OF THE WAYS THAT WOMEN HAVE ENDED UP FEELING BADLY ABOUT THEMSELVES

Women will need to work systematically at reclaiming feeling good about themselves. Gender conditioning, by defining the characteristics of a 'real woman', confronts each woman with how she fails to live up to the definition. This causes feelings of inadequacy and self-criticism. Low self-esteem is a terrible burden – women may end up not trusting their own judgement, always seeing the worst in themselves and, in some way, setting up situations so that failure is more likely.

The most important contradiction to feeling badly about oneself is to begin the task of reclaiming one's self-esteem. Women can decide that they will not spend time worrying about the 'right way' of doing things, begin to notice what they do well and refuse to listen to inappropriate criticism. They can have fun appreciating themselves. Many women report that it is helpful to undertake self-appreciation without limit or reservation and to continue to do so every day, especially at times when one is feeling self-critical or is being criticized.

THE DECISION TO APPRECIATE ONESELF

I now decide to appreciate myself just as I am without limit or reservation. I do not need to compare myself with any set of criteria about how a woman should behave or with any other woman. I am enough just as I am!

I will write further on the function and process of self-appreciation in rebuilding self-esteem in Chapter 11 and on how to undertake it in Chapter 12.

CHALLENGING ALL OF THE WAYS THAT WOMEN HAVE ENDED UP FEELING BADLY TOWARDS OTHER WOMEN

One of the most pernicious effects of internalized sexism is the way in which it divides women and sets them against one another. The criteria and standards for what it takes to be a 'real woman' are often installed in women's minds by their being compared adversely (and sometimes positively) with other women. This has the effect of conditioning many women to keep their eye on how other women look and behave, to be 'judgemental' about them and to compete to see who is the best at meeting the characteristics of a 'real woman'.

Consequently, relationships between women can sometimes become characterized by what may be termed 'bitchiness'. By this I mean small-minded antagonisms and put-downs of one another. It may also lead to women not acting with integrity towards one another, since they see themselves as competitors, perhaps for the attention of a man or for a job.

It is in the nature of the oppressive society that the content of how women feel badly towards one another is often rooted in prejudice or negative stereotypes about the group to which another woman belongs. Thus, bad feelings towards a black woman are simply racism at work; bad feelings towards a lesbian are heterosexism; and bad feelings towards a woman with a disability are able-bodiedism. These oppressive attitudes are just as endemic between women as any other group, and need careful work to eliminate.

Clearly, feeling badly towards another woman is only possible if a woman is first feeling badly towards herself, and much of the criticism of other women is rooted in the same criticisms of oneself. Whenever I feel badly about me, I am likely to feel critical of you.

Challenging all of these aspects of internalized sexism requires a two step approach. These are:

O   First, to recognize that bad feelings towards other women, regardless of what reason is given for holding them, are not 'natural' but are the product of oppression and gender conditioning.

O   Second, to decide to not act on those feelings, but to reach to treat every other women with complete respect regardless of how she behaves.

THE DECISION TO TREAT EVERY OTHER WOMAN WITH COMPLETE RESPECT

I decide that I will treat every other woman with complete respect regardless of how she behaves towards me or how I may feel about her behaviour.

Making this decision does not mean that a woman should allow other women to mistreat her, and there will be circumstances where it is necessary to insist that no such mistreatment takes place. However, there is an important difference between not giving up on someone as a person regardless of how they behave and still not allowing them to mistreat us. In taking complete charge of our situation as leaders, we are all challenged to protect ourselves from mistreatment while holding onto a belief in the inherent nature of other people and treating them accordingly.

CHALLENGING ALL OF THE WAYS THAT WOMEN MISTREAT THEMSELVES

Internalized oppression causes women to mistreat themselves in a variety of ways. If the most extreme form of misogyny (hatred of women) present in our society is internalized, then a woman may severely abuse herself mentally or physically Even lower levels of self-disgust can lead to a variety of eating disorders such as anorexia nervosa or bulimia. Equally, having plastic surgery when it is not a medical necessity in order to improve how one looks seems to me to be a kind of unnecessary self-abuse.

It is only possible to begin to mistreat oneself if one has lost a sense of one's own value. The effects of oppression are always to reduce the sense people have of how good they are, how well they do and how much they have to offer. For women, this is particularly powerful and the key contradiction seems to be to reclaim a sense of one's inherent value and, on that basis, to decide to never again mistreat oneself in any way whatsoever.

THE DECISION TO NEVER MISTREAT ONESELF AGAIN

I promise to remember that I am valuable beyond measure and I decide that I will never abuse myself again or put myself down in any way whatsoever, however badly I feel.

CHALLENGING ALL OF THE WAYS THAT WOMEN MISTREAT OTHER WOMEN

If people mistreat themselves, they will probably mistreat other people. This is the basic mechanism of oppression at work. In any place where we have internalized feeling badly about, and therefore agree to mistreat, ourselves we will be prone to mistreat someone else in our own group in the forlorn hope of feeling better.

The previously mentioned notion of one woman putting another down, termed as 'being bitchy', is a good example of this process at work. This might take the form of making sarcastic comments to another woman's face or behind her back, but it is always based in self-criticism. We attack others for aspects of their appearance or behaviour that we are insecure about in ourselves.

The ultimate challenge here is to decide to build a close dependable relationship with every other woman and to plan to never again mistreat any woman in any way whatsoever.

THE DECISION TO NEVER AGAIN MISTREAT ANY OTHER WOMAN

I decide to never again mistreat any other woman in any way whatsoever, but instead to reach to build the best possible relationship I can based upon cooperation, mutual respect and support.

CHALLENGING ALL OF THE WAYS THAT WOMEN ALLOW THEMSELVES TO BE MISTREATED

Mistreatment comes in the first instance from the outside. Each of us was born with our inherent nature intact, unless we have pre-frontal brain damage, and only after we were mistreated as children did we begin to accept the messages and behaviour that oppression brings.

Therefore, in thinking about how to challenge the ways in which women allow themselves to be mistreated we must begin by tackling sexism itself. The decision to see to it that absolutely everything goes well must include the eradication of oppression and its effects. Discrimination is unjust and operates to reduce the overall effectiveness of every organization. Prejudice damages both the perpetrator and the recipient. Challenging patterns of oppression is often uncomfortable for people and in particular for men, but it is an essential step towards fully reclaiming power. The way in which sexism places men, as a group, in 'control' must also be challenged both at the personal and at the institutional level.

The international women's liberation movement has played a key role in campaigning against sexism and continues to offer many women the support and direction they need to maintain their efforts. Many women disassociate themselves from the movement because they believe the prejudice expressed about it by the media, but in my experience most women agree with its objectives.

There is presently much debate about the campaign to eliminate inappropriate language or behaviour from our institutions by establishing guidelines. Language is a very important 'purveyor' of sexism and changing our language is a significant step in its elimination. In my view, the attack on language guidelines because they are rooted in 'political correctness' is, in the main, another example of prejudice at work rather than a well thought out discussion of the issues. While it is always possible that, in the pursuit of equality, the members of any oppressed group may move into attacking the people who have been their oppressors, eliminating sexism from men's behaviour will require a giant step, particularly on the part of men. It is a huge and often painful process and resistance can take many simple and complex forms – arguing about 'political correctness' is one form aimed at reducing very important issues to the mundane.

Challenging the way in which women agree to be mistreated also means that women will need to challenge all forms of harassment and sexual harassment, and support one another in doing so. Harassment at work puts women in constant fear for their safety and thereby reduces their willingness to take visible leadership. Sexual harassment, while apparently having a 'sexual' content, is simply another attempt at control and thus has to be opposed. In particular, this means breaking the silence about sexual harassment in the workplace. While this silence is completely understandable, it has often allowed just one man to continue the harassment of many women over many years.

The key contradiction is for women to decide to take themselves completely seriously. Women deserve to be treated well in every situation and everyone needs to encourage them to remember it. Moreover, women need to move on from this point to deciding to never again agree to be mistreated in any way whatsoever and to reclaim their power and take charge.

THE DECISION TO NEVER AGAIN AGREE TO ACCEPT MISTREATMENT IN ANY FORM WHATSOEVER

I deserve to be treated well in all situations. I decide that I will never again agree to accept any mistreatment but will act powerfuly instead to take charge fully of whatever situation I am in.

CHALLENGING ALL OF THE WAYS THAT WOMEN ALLOW OTHER WOMEN TO BE MISTREATED

One of the biggest hurts that all young people suffer is having to stand by and watch other young people being mistreated. The fear of being hurt myself if I were to attempt to stop something, coupled with the feeling of guilt and powerlessness because I did nothing, creates a great deal of internal confusion. This is especially difficult for women because so much of their conditioning communicates that women are dependent on someone else for protection and are unable to take charge of things themselves.

It is therefore vital that women stand up for other women, both individually and as a group, and encourage them to stand up for themselves. Women will need to work together with other women and with men to eliminate all mistreatment of women.

THE DECISION TO NEVER AGAIN ALLOW ANY OTHER WOMAN TO BE MISTREATED

I decide to be an ally to every other woman in their efforts to eliminate all mistreatment of themselves, by standing up for them and supporting them to stand up for themselves.

WOMEN SETTLING FOR LESS

In Chapter 6 I argued that the core of women's internalized oppression is agreeing to settle for less in their lives, in their work and in their leadership. The biggest challenge is to begin the process of deciding to settle for nothing less than absolutely everything, and to plan how to overcome all of the obstacles to achieving it. Many women have found it helpful to make the decision over and over while reviewing the consequences as they go.

DECIDING TO SETTLE FOR NOTHING LESS THAN ABSOLUTELY EVERYTHING

A woman begins by saying out loud:
    'I promise that from now on I will never again settle for anything less than absolutely everything in my life and my leadership!'

She then asks herself:
'What is the implication of this decision? What does this mean I will need to do next?'

She may wish to write down her thoughts as the basis for an action plan.

She then makes the decision several times, each time thinking about what it would mean she would do. She continues in this process for as long as makes sense.

WORKING ON THE DECISION IN A WOMEN-ONLY GROUP

Women may wish to experiment with making the decision in the company of other women. If a number of women work together, the group can pay one woman attention while she makes the decision. They can cheer her on as she contemplates how this will change her life and her leadership. When she has taken a turn, another woman can use the attention of the group to make the same decision.

At first, it may be hard to take the process seriously, and many women become frightened that they are promising to do something that is too big and they will subsequently fail at it. However, I think this is a misunderstanding of the process. The intention is not to make binding decisions but to give oneself the opportunity to contemplate what it would mean if one took it seriously, what one would change and how much one really wants.

To keep with the decision will require plenty of encouragement, and it is important to value every thought that comes even if, at first, they seem insignificant or too 'selfish'. As a woman continues, the process will deepen and gradually she will begin to deal with the most important concerns of her life.

BUILDING A PROGRAMME FROM THE DECISIONS

The decisions I have proposed can be developed and used as part of a complete programme for women's leadership development. When working with individual women or with a group, the decisions can form the basis for a systematic approach. Put them together on one sheet as opposite.

O   I now decide to appreciate myself just as I am without limit or reservation. I do not need to compare myself with any set of criteria about how a woman should behave or with any other woman. I am enough just as I am!

O   I decide that I will treat every other woman with complete respect regardless of how she behaves towards me or how I may feel about her behaviour.

O   I promise to remember that I am valuable beyond measure and I decide that I will never ever mistreat myself again in any way whatsoever, however badly I feel.

O   I decide to never again mistreat any other woman in any way whatsoever, but instead to reach to build the best possible relationship I can based upon cooperation, mutual respect and support.

O   I deserve to be treated well in all situations. I decide that I will never again accept mistreatment but will act powerfully instead to take charge fully of whatever situation I am in.

O   I decide to be an ally to every other woman in their efforts to eliminate all mistreatment of themselves by standing up for them and in supporting them to stand up for themselves.

O   I promise that from now on I will never again settle for anything less than absolutely everything in my leadership!

8

UNDERSTANDING MEN'S GENDER CONDITIONING

❖

Men occupy most of the key leadership positions in the world – in national government, in local government, in business, in trade unions and in local organizations. In the developed countries of the first world, it is mostly white, able-bodied men who occupy these positions. Although women have made some advances, the statistics in Chapter 6 (see p. 65) demonstrate that men are still chosen for formal leadership positions in greater numbers than women. The number of women in managerial positions has actually begun to decline again in the first years of the 1990s.

If the key determinants of organizational values and culture are the attitudes and behaviour of the people in key leadership positions, and if the people in those key leadership positions are men, then organizational culture will inevitably have a predominantly 'maasculine' feel, and this will determine the leadership style of incoming or upcoming leaders whether they are women or men.

These 'masculine' values and behaviours have great strengths. For example, men tend to have a high commitment to achievement, determination to get things done whatever the costs, and enormous intelligence and skill.

However, the economic crisis of recent years, and the rapid changes in people's attitudes described in Chapter 1, have meant that organizations, if they are to survive, must begin to place people at the heart of everything they do. They must develop a process that enables them to become an inclusive organization, striving to include everyone in every aspect of how the enterprise functions.

People in formal leadership positions must create the ideal conditions for this inside the organization. They must place the highest value on the contribution that can be made by the people who work for them, and work to build close, dependable relationships with them; they must be prepared to develop shared goals and be dedicated to developing a process of innovation and continual improvement throughout the organization. Above all, they must be committed to pursuing cooperation at all levels – between individuals, within teams and between groups and departments.

These attributes are often less well developed in men than women, and particularly in men who are chosen to lead in organizations that base their approach on traditional leadership; the way that men are brought up tends to make them aggressive, task- and achievement-orientated, self-centred and competitive. Moreover, men with these attributes are likely to select men like themselves for new leadership positions or for their own replacements. This means that the leadership that most men are conditioned to provide is no longer appropriate to the needs of organizations during the remaining years of this century.

If we are to make changes in how men lead we first have to understand why men behave in this way. I am particularly indebted to Charlie Kreiner for his contribution in systematically mapping out this area of our thinking.

WHAT HAPPENS TO MEN?

I believe that there is a general and almost universal anti-male conditioning in this society. It portrays men as less than fully human, and therefore expendable and exploitable, to be used by society as a whole for its own purposes. As the old song says, men are made of 'slugs and snails and puppy dogs' tails'. It is as though it does not really matter what their lives are like, after all, they are 'only men', and this is how men are expected to be. Men are treated as beasts of burden, expected to be breadwinners, trained as warriors, and expected to behave as though 'they will go out of control' at any moment.

If oppression is 'the one-way, systematic and institutionalized mistreatment of one group of people either by another group acting as the agents of society as a whole or by society as a whole', as defined in Chapter 5, then we can say that men are, in their own right, an oppressed group. However, no other group oppresses men as such; indeed, it is very important in speaking of men's oppression, to state clearly that men are oppressed but not by women or children. An individual woman may mistreat an individual man and an individual man may well feel mistreated, but there is no systematic, one-way institutionalized mistreatment. The force of law does not say that such treatment is acceptable and there is no consensus of agreement that 'it's all right for women to mistreat men in this way'.

We can say, therefore, that men are an oppressed group, but oppressed by society as a whole. In practice, a great deal of the mistreatment is done by men towards men; fathers towards sons, older brothers towards younger brothers, male teachers towards male students, friends to one another, and so on.

WHY OPPRESS MEN?

What does society gain from the less than fully human treatment of men? The 'purpose' that men's oppression seems to serve is to encourage, train and prepare men to act as:

O   Hunters and warriors;
O   Breadwinners and wage workers;
O   Agents of sexism towards women.

HUNTERS AND WARRIORS

Since pre-history, men in many societies have been brought up to become hunters and warriors. There have been many societies where women have played that role, not least that of the Amazon, but these have all been replaced over time with patriarchal cultures in which the men have played the more predominant and aggressive role.

Being a hunter or warrior used to be dangerous; there are always risks from those we fight or hunt, either during or even after the confrontation. In order to prepare male children for this role they had to be made to feel and behave as though it is permissible for their lives to be expendable.

Also, men have to be conditioned to be the aggressors and the defenders; each young male is either brutalized and humiliated or made afraid that he will be. He is taught, often at an unconscious or unaware level, that 'real men' will agree to kill or be killed by their brothers as a fundamental condition of their maleness.

IF ROLES WERE REVERSED?

Imagine how things would be if it were women rather than men who were brought up 'to kill or be killed in the name of their manhood'?

What would have to be done to women to get their agreement to 'kill or be killed' in the name of their womanhood?

How would women feel about men if it was only women who were brought up to kill or be killed, if it was always 'men and children first'?

How would women feel about other women if each knew that the other was brought up to kill or be killed in the name of their womanhood?

It may seem unthinkable, but it is exactly what is expected of each male!

Quoted from Charlie Kreiner, Men's Liberation Leader, USA

BREADWINNERS AND WAGE WORKERS

Men are expected to 'produce' more income than they need just to support themselves. Historically, they have been trained to take on the role of sole breadwinner, while women have been given the role of sole parent, cook and housekeeper. It has been men's job to provide economic security for the family and men often become uncomfortable when they are not at work producing something.

This has limited the lives of most men to that of wage worker. You often hear men say to their children, 'I'm not doing it for myself, I'm doing it for you and your mother'. Men tend to 'blame' their family for their 'imprisonment' in a job that, for most of them, has probably never been a positive choice anyway. Men are brought up to be primarily concerned with 'doing' and achievement at the expense of their relationships with other people and regardless of their own preferences or best interests as human beings.

AGENTS OF SEXISM TOWARDS WOMEN

Men are raised within a culture that is dominated by discrimination and prejudice towards women. This society teaches every person, male and female alike, that women are both special and to be treasured, and second-class citizens of less value than men. It teaches that the work men do is important and exciting (and it sometimes is) and what women do is inferior, boring and to be avoided at all costs (which it sometimes is, but where it involves caring for young people full time, is of enormous value). It teaches that women are not as clever or able as men, that they will need men's protection, and that their correct place is to work in the home, look after a family and satisfy men's needs.

Since this communication about women takes place at the same time as men are being conditioned to be modern hunters and breadwinners, they will be tempted to collude with the notion of their superiority in order to feel better about themselves. This is the cycle of oppression at work. Men are conditioned to accept the mistreatment that is done to them and then pass it on to women.

In recent years, a gradual change has been occurring in which more women are staying in or returning to the workforce, and a few are reaching significant positions of leadership. This does not appear to be the result of a positive move on the part of employers towards equality of opportunity, but is motivated by a desire to reduce labour costs by employing cheaper labour (women!) or more part-time staff (women!). However, even though there are more women in the workforce, while the underlying prejudice remains about women's role, women still have to undertake the vast majority of work in the home as well as maintaining a full time job.

WHAT IS THE CONTENT OF MEN'S GENDER CONDITIONING?

Central to the process of conditioning men is the requirement to behave like a 'real man'. I believe that people begin life completely 'satisfied' with themselves as female or male human beings and they 'expect' others to be completely 'satisfied' too. In order to condition men for their future role in society, however, it is necessary to establish a number of attributes and behaviours that describe a 'real man', which we can call the 'masculine stereotype'. This stereotype is then used as the basis for a comparison with the way that men actually behave – and men are always found wanting.

Exercise 8.1   Masculine stereotypes

Take a sheet of paper and pen and write down all the stereotypes you were brought up to expect from 'real men'. Here is a start: 'Real men' are strong, silent, unemotional, fearless, tall, dark and handsome, reliable ...

Then write down how you feel when men do not behave according to the stereotype.

The process of male conditioning takes place while growing up and occurs in a number of very specific ways. Some of the most important of these are the following:

O   Men have to be disconnected from their ability to feel.
O   Men are separated from women by sexism.
O   All men are hurt by gay oppression and homophobia.
O   All men are the victims of violence and abuse.
O   Men become isolated and achievement-orientated.
O   Women become sexual objects.
O   Men are separated from their children by work.

Figure 8.1, on page 88, illustrates some of these points.

MEN HAVE TO BE DISCONNECTED FROM THEIR ABILITY TO FEEL

The stereotype of a 'real man' begins with the notion that real men are strong, know what they are doing, and are never weak or vulnerable. Their ability to feel, be in touch with their feelings and discharge when necessary has to be damaged if they are to achieve the status of 'real men'. They are told to 'take it like a man', 'don't ever be scared of anything' and 'big boys don't cry'.

These instructions are almost always accompanied by the threat or reality of violence for non-compliance. If boys continue to cry, they are told, 'If you don't stop crying I'll give you something to cry about'. If they come home and say they were 'beaten up', they might be hit for losing and forced to go out and fight again.

Now, it is true that many female children are also told not to cry and can be hit or threatened, but the key difference is that with male children an explicit connection is made between the injunction not to cry and their making it as 'real men'.

In time men internalize the mistreatment, ridicule others who cry and choke back their own feelings to avoid further abuse. Gradually, they lose touch with how they feel and then with how others feel. They lose their inherent human compassion and tenderness, particularly with one another. They often find it hard to be easy in ordinary human relationships and the relationships they do have can be quite superficial. As a part of this, they can lose or inhibit their ability to love deeply and receive love – how can anyone who has been treated this way be lovable?

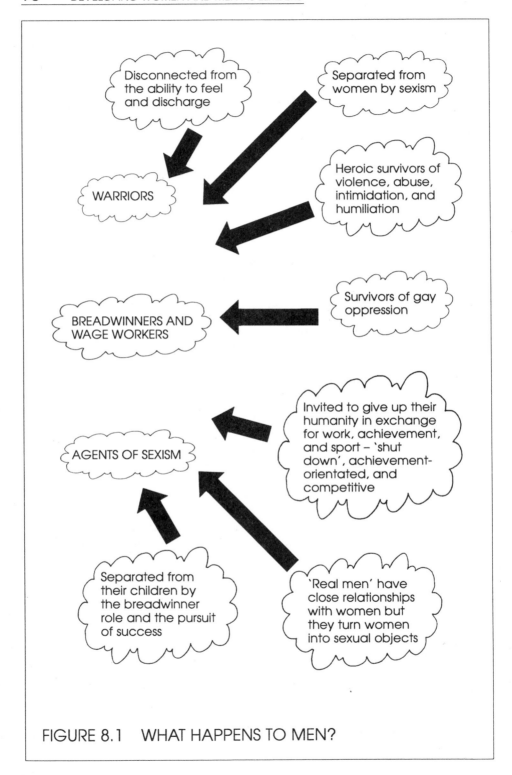

FIGURE 8.1   WHAT HAPPENS TO MEN?

They are now vulnerable to being conditioned to put work and action ahead of how they feel.

LEARNING TO IGNORE HOW YOU FEEL

A man attending a leadership training programme for men spoke recently of his experience of violence and the fear of becoming emotional at school. 'I was caned in front of the whole school for something I hadn't done and I had to bite my lips and pray that I would not start to cry in front of my mates. You were the toughest boy if you behaved as though you felt nothing.'

While not all men have experiences quite like the example above, many do and most of the rest see it happening to their friends. There is great pressure to agree to keep feelings repressed rather than letting them show and risking the condemnation of others. This is an important aspect of the internalized oppression of men.

MEN ARE SEPARATED FROM WOMEN BY SEXISM

As described earlier, the sexist culture in which we live communicates to boys and girls that it is better to be male than female. Males will have more exciting lives, receive more respect, and will have greater opportunities. Boys are serious and girls are 'silly', boys are tough and girls are soft, boys are more dependable and girls are emotional. As a consequence, many boys end up feeling completely contemptuous of girls, terrified of associating or being associated with them.

The effect of this is to divide boys from girls. For example, some little boys will draw away from their mothers rather than be seen on the streets with them; they will avoid playing or being seen with little girls in their neighbourhood; they will ridicule and humiliate girls in their school. This is sexism and while it is clearly a terrible hurt and extremely damaging to women, it is, in fact, a tragedy for young males too; to agree at any level to treat another human being as in any way inferior to one's self is a hurt that rebounds repeatedly in the lives of adult men.

However, the immediate effect is to create the feeling that 'real men' should live lives that are isolated and self-sufficient. It begins to re-enforce the isolation and loneliness that is such a feature of most men's lives.

ALL MEN ARE HURT BY GAY OPPRESSION AND HOMOPHOBIA

Gay oppression plays a crucial role in conditioning men to behave within the limits of the stereotype of the 'real man'. It is used to create a class of men who 'make it' and a class of men who do not make it. 'Real men' are unemotional, tough, and tireless, like Rambo; they are able to 'take' the mistreatment aimed at men without showing any feelings. 'Non-real men' are those who are unable to 'take' the mistreatment, and are then abused not only by those who initiate it but by their compatriots who continue the mistreatment. They are then described as 'sissy' or with the put-downs of gay oppression, such as 'poofy'.

This process is at its strongest in boys from around the age of 7 onwards. It creates three groups – 'real men', women and 'non-real men'. First, boys are made contemptuous of females and then they are made contemptuous of other males who are unable to 'make the grade'. This is the beginning of gay oppression.

While gay men suffer gay oppression in cruel and devastating ways, all men experience the oppression as a mechanism for limiting their relationships with one another. While the general justification for gay oppression is the sexual behaviour of gay men, in fact it has nothing whatsoever to do with sexuality; its real purpose is to divide men and set them against one another.

Gay oppression effectively eliminates the possibility of most men having close, dependable relationships with one another. The core component is fear. Most men are terrified of getting close to other men; most males are terrified of being thought gay by other men; most males are terrified of associating with gay men. This fear is often called 'homophobia' and it fuels gay oppression. The jokes on the radio or television, the discrimination and violence, the underlying scorn society holds for gay men, restrict the freedom of all men to build warm, co-operative, loving relationships with other men in their lives in general and at work.

ALL MEN ARE THE VICTIMS OF VIOLENCE AND ABUSE

Watch boys playing together in the playground. Their lives are surrounded by violence or the fear of violence, especially at school. If we listen to older men tell the story of their early lives, we will hear countless examples of deliberate and systematic brutality and humiliation. In one secondary school, for example, the gym master would hit every boy on the legs with a slipper as they left the gym for no rational reason. Other men have spoken of being made to hold a medicine ball above their heads or the gym master turning the showers from hot to cold and then back again while he watched. The ones that can take it become the 'real men', while the rest are abused and laughed at, not least by other boys.

The toys that are bought for boys, and often most treasured, are those that enable them to rehearse war. In my own youth games involved guns and playing 'Cowboys and Indians', but the present-day equivalent involves using the range of increasingly violent computer software that is available. It is clear that 'real men' know how to fight and do not flinch from the challenge.

They then have the choice of either becoming a 'traditional male' and shutting down their feelings, or joining the group of men who 'don't make it'. This latter group often becomes identified as the emerging 'gay group' and faces a possible lifetime of discrimination, prejudice and separation from most other males as a consequence.

In the extreme this mistreatment conditions men for their role as warriors. They find it difficult to be in touch with how hurt they may feel themselves or how much their behaviour is hurting others. It all becomes a matter of fact, just something you have to do and then live with; but in reality it leaves men permanently frightened when they are in the company of other men and a great deal of bravado is needed in order to cope.

MEN BECOME ISOLATED AND ACHIEVEMENT-ORIENTATED

Here, I am thinking of boys aged about 11. The first effect of this conditioning has been to disconnect them from their feelings. Second, it makes relationships with females extremely difficult. Subsequently, as the fear of gay oppression increases, they also avoid close relationships with other young men. They often become desperately lonely, but are unable to talk to anyone about how they feel because 'real men don't talk about their feelings'.

To 'replace' their inherent connection to themselves and their natural desire for closeness and contact with women and other men alike, men are encouraged to accept work, money and achievement as a substitute. They are taught and pressured into an increasing concern with getting results through individual initiative rather than by working with other people. They learn to put their feelings to one side while they dedicate themselves to the task. Since there is no place that they can take their feelings, they have to decide to try to 'get on' in life as a way of feeling better about themselves. Their approach is based on win–lose and competition rather than win–win through cooperation.

Since men dominate the formal leadership of most organizations, this leads those organizations to take on a 'results-orientated' culture based upon 'traditional leadership'.

WOMEN BECOME SEXUAL OBJECTS

Having been separated from females through most of their early years, as they become teenagers men are taught that 'real men' do have relationships with women after all. However, they are now told that the purpose of these relationships is not companionship or intimacy, but 'having sex', and, since they have already been told that females are second class, they are bound to see them as objects rather than real people with real feelings. Young women become the target of sexual attention driven on by the need of men to brag about their deeds in order to avoid ridicule from others.

This is not caused by the inherent nature of the male, neither is it the adolescent arousal of the sex drive; it is the inevitable consequence of the oppression of women and men. Young men, lonely and isolated and under constant pressure from their friends to 'perform', begin to build relationships with young women who have, themselves, been conditioned to believe that their role with a man is to do what they are told and to make him happy. Inevitably, the prime concern of men becomes, 'How far will she go?'.

All this leaves young men often confused and feeling inadequate about their relationships with women. On the one hand, desperate for closeness and warmth and on the other, judging themselves on their sexual prowess. Of course, as they become adults, most men work to build excellent relationships with women.

However, this legacy can create an underlying and justified fear of sexual harassment for many women that lasts a lifetime. It is often reinforced by the behaviour of some men in the workplace who make constant innuendoes and sometimes sexual advances.

MEN ARE SEPARATED FROM THEIR CHILDREN BY WORK

Even today, most men and women in heterosexual relationships who become parents still end up agreeing that the woman should leave the workforce to look after the children. This is a product of continuing cultural pressure and expectations placed on both partners, and an economic situation that still rewards men with higher incomes than women in most cases. Moreover, many people who plan to have children, do so just at a time when the pressures on the man to do well at work are increasing.

There are very few work situations where there is a relaxed and understanding attitude to the importance of children, and given the attitudes that exist about childcare being 'women's work', it is often hard for a man to give the priority to being with and looking after his children that they deserve. As a result, men are often separated from their young ones during their earliest years, leaving for work before the children are up or returning after they have gone to bed. At weekends men may feel that they 'deserve' a break and they will go out alone or with their friends to participate in sport or entertainment.

Over recent years, however, men have been increasingly unable to earn sufficient money to keep a family at an acceptable standard of living, leading to an increasing number of women returning to work soon after the birth of their child. In most cases, women continue to be the ones undertaking the care of the children and the bulk of the domestic duties as well. This leaves men still in the traditional situation of being separated from their children.

All in all, this is a great hurt to men, leaving them isolated from one of the most important and nourishing experiences possible in their lives. Today, many men are aware of these tensions and are working hard to overcome the separation, but this itself can bring increased stress.

ADDING IT ALL UP

By the time they are grown up, men seem to be 'booby-trapped' for life, few ever feeling that they make it as 'real men'. Underneath the veneer of confidence and pretension that many men adopt, they are insecure and uncertain. This is male internalized oppression and it comprises all of the ways in which men 'agree' to reduce their own human value in exchange for doing things within the limits of the traditional male role.

However, in a society dominated by sexism, individual men are frequently offered the possibility of taking on more than their 'fair share' of leadership opportunities in comparison with women. These leadership positions, in a predominantly 'male culture', then encourage men to act confidently, get on, not talk about their feelings, and to work long hours.

Some of the worst characteristics of organizations that are dominated by this culture include the following:

O   People driving themselves in an atmosphere of 'success whatever the cost'.
O   Intense competition to see who is best at anything and everything.
O   Constant abuse and criticism behind people's backs.
O   A complete lack of mutual support and respect, typified by ridicule and put downs.
O   People are expected still to be at work long after official working hours.
O   People will feel under intense pressure and some may resort to heavy smoking or drinking to cope.

This 'male culture' is dominant in all kinds of organizations, from the military, police, engineering and motor industry to white-collar organizations such as the civil service, building societies and insurance companies. In reality, it is the same 'traditional leadership' culture described in Chapter 2; apparently, the gender conditioning of men is a key underlying determinant of the whole culture.

MEN'S GENDER CONDITIONING INHIBITS EFFECTIVE LEADERSHIP

The gender conditioning of men is a key hindrance to their effective leadership. It means that when they lead they often feel as though they have to behave like 'real men' and as a consequence, they think they have to be fearless, tireless, never need help from anyone else, take little interest in other people as people and know everything! This means that, in reality, they are less than fully suitable for the job. Most men have been, quite simply, trained in the wrong approach, emphasizing all the traits that are least likely to bring success because they restrict the possibility of others giving of their best.

I have examined in some detail the most important determinants of the behaviour of men as leaders in organizations. Let us now consider what is required if men are to become effective as leaders in their own right, and if they are to become effective allies for one another and for women in building an inclusive organization.

9

DEVELOPING A NEW LEADERSHIP FOR MEN

❖

The situation facing men as leaders in organizations requires that they make a fundamental change in the approach they have traditionally adopted to leadership. The leadership style of most men is no longer appropriate. I demonstrated in Chapter 8 that the way men typically lead in the present situation is a consequence of the gender conditioning they receive when they are growing up and the expectations placed upon them as adult men and as workers in organizations.

In a society in which men are more highly valued than women, the values, behaviour, and therefore cultures that predominate in organizations are those held, introduced and maintained by men. To reach the top in such an organization, men have often had to be ambitious, power-driven and ruthless and once at the top they have traditionally selected men who behave like themselves for promotion to new leadership positions. This maintains a 'real man' culture in most organizations simply through the sheer numbers of men in senior positions.

In many situations, women are still regarded as less able and therefore less worthy of recruitment, promotion or training, except perhaps in particular skill ghettos. Where women are promoted to leadership they are often those women whose values and style are acceptable to their male bosses. However, when they behave 'like men' in going about their work, they are often criticized for being 'hard nosed and uncaring'. Apparently, they lose out whatever happens!

Therefore, as I described in Chapter 2, if we are to build inclusive organizations, we need leaders who are able to think beyond their own ideas to encourage the contribution and abilities of others. In the case of men, this means being able to encourage and support women's leadership in the face of institutional discrimination and prejudice. This requires flexibility, openness and sensitivity in order to be able to build close, dependable relationships with people who have different perspectives and varied backgrounds.

CREATING A NEW MEN'S LEADERSHIP

Work with men as leaders to undo the effects of men's gender conditioning is a priority if organizations are to make a fresh, new and accurate response to these rapidly changing times. Thus, we must create a new leadership for men; men will need to examine how they have been conditioned and trained to behave and then plan how to overcome the conditioning.

It may seem strange to talk of 'creating a new men's leadership'; after all, men have always had a great deal of attention paid to them. As I have said, men still hold most of the formal leadership positions and most of the training and management development initiated in organizations since the 1960s has been given to men. Nevertheless, if we are to improve the effectiveness of men's leadership and help them become effective allies with women to change the culture of the organization, we must target action at men in their own right.

This new leadership will be based on men developing and using all of their existing strengths, such as a high commitment to achievement, determination to get things done, and enormous intelligence and skills; but also reclaiming those abilities that are not generally highly developed among men, such as thinking with real vision, and their natural cooperativeness, sensitivity and commitment to treating themselves and others well.

To do this we need to help men begin to make changes that will contradict the ways in which they have internalized men's oppression. The first step is to help them begin the process of making a fundamental change in their image of what a 'real man' is and then putting that revised view at the centre of how they live their lives.

They will need to apply it first to how they treat themselves, second in how they treat other men, and third in how they treat women.

MEN MAKING CHANGES IN HOW THEY TREAT THEMSELVES

There are three main contradictions that men need to address when examining how they treat themselves. They are the following:

O   Men need to learn how to value themselves and be in touch with their own goodness.

O   Men need to learn how to talk about their doubts, concerns and anxieties rather than keeping a stiff upper lip.

O   Men need to decide to give up overworking and other symptoms of self-abuse.

VALUING THEMSELVES AND BEING IN TOUCH WITH THEIR OWN GOODNESS

Men will need to contradict the feeling that their lives are not important because they are 'beasts of burden' who are dispensable and exploitable. The lives of all men are valuable and every man is inherently good. Like everyone else, men will not get everything right, but at the inherent level when the whole situation is taken into account they have done the very best they can and therefore deserve neither reproach nor blame. This means that they will need to learn how to appreciate themselves, including appreciating themselves just as they are right now, warts and all.

A COMMITMENT TO REMEMBERING THAT ONE IS VALUABLE BEYOND MEASURE

In order to increase their sense of self-worth and value, men can practise deciding:

'From now on I decide that I will at all times remember I am a good man and that I am valuable beyond measure.'

A good approach to undertaking self-appreciation is described in detail in Chapter 12.

MEN NEED TO TALK ABOUT THEIR DOUBTS, CONCERNS AND ANXIETIES

'Real men' don't talk about their feelings and concerns with anyone, even their partners or best friends. In their leadership this can result in the pretence that everything is fine when in fact it is not, but offers of help at this point are usually rejected. I will return to this topic later in the chapter in terms of the way men control their feelings in their relationships with women and propose a decision that men can take to contradict this aspect of their gender conditioning.

MEN NEED TO DECIDE TO GIVE UP OVERWORKING AND OTHER SYMPTOMS OF SELF-ABUSE

Men must be encouraged to explore how to give up overworking or abusing themselves physically in any way. The training to overwork begins early in their lives with the conditioning that they are merely 'beasts of burden'. They will need to learn how to put their own human well-being at the centre of their leadership, taking on the notion that 'It is important to treat myself well – my life matters!', rather than acting on the feeling of 'a man has got to do what a man has got to do!'. Any place where men feel as though they have to grit their teeth and keep on going regardless of their own needs or those of others are likely to be places where internalized oppression is operating.

ELIMINATING THE PATTERN OF OVERWORK AS A LEADER

Men can experiment with making the decision to end the habit of overworking by practising saying and deciding that:

'From now on I will assume that this organization needs me fit, rested and healthy and that it is possible to do my job without overworking. I therefore now decide that I will never again behave in any way that is designed to prove to others that I am tough, tougher or the toughest.'

And then adding all of the things that would logically follow if they were to do that. Men could then experiment with putting the ideas they come up with into practice in their leadership for a trial period, such as a week.

MAKING CHANGES IN HOW MEN TREAT OTHER MEN

The challenge to men in creating a new leadership is to root it fiercely in close, dependable and respectful relationships with every other person at work, whether she or he is boss, peer, subordinate or in a totally different organization. This is particularly difficult for men to do with other men.

The basic mechanism that keeps men acting within the limits of men's gender conditioning is their fear of what other men will think or do if they do not. Gay oppression plays an important role in men's oppression by installing a deep fear of closeness between men, which I have called 'homophobia'. This encourages men to keep their relationships with one another superficial and instrumental.

As a result, men often 'play out' their internalized oppression in the workplace through 'put downs' and banter towards other men which those other men are expected to accept and join in with in kind. Sometimes, this takes the form of telling jokes, sometimes it includes ridiculing other men behind their backs or it can take the form of racist behaviour towards a black man or a disrespectful attitude towards a disabled man.

Men need to overcome this by deciding to befriend every other man, to strive for respect and understanding and to create an alliance with them to change the organization as a whole.

BUILDING CLOSE ALLIANCES WITH OTHER MEN

Men can practise deciding:

'I decide to work together with every other man in friendship and cooperation, striving for respect and mutual trust and never again agreeing to treat other men as competitors or enemies in any way whatsoever.'

MAKING CHANGES IN HOW MEN TREAT WOMEN

Those of us who have been working with men as leaders during the past ten years have always been committed to the elimination of sexism and the creation of organizations in which women are able to take their rightful place in leadership. During that time we have mainly focused our work on tackling and improving the way men treat themselves and other men as I have described above. This practice was based on an assumption that if men were able to challenge and effectively tackle their own oppression first, they would then tackle sexism.

Great progress has been made with this work. Many men have been able to build significant numbers of relationships with other men in their personal lives and at work which are based upon respect, trust and mutual cooperation. Clearly, this has been and will continue to be essential if men are to move on to the work they need to do to eliminate sexism.

However, the assumption that this would be sufficient on its own has not been borne out. The evidence suggests that it has not led to a big improvement in how men treat individual women; indeed sometimes it has even made matters worse, with men blaming the women they are closest to for not providing them with as good support as provided by their new found, close men friends.

It also seems to have been less then fully effective in mobilizing men to challenge and work towards eliminating institutional sexism. Men often assume that sexism is an interpersonal issue rather than the one-way, systematic and institutionalized mistreatment of women by men, where men are acting as the agents of society as a whole. This has sometimes led to a situation whereby men merely try not to behave 'in a sexist manner', opting for a kind of 'behaviour modification programme' in which they have taken their sexist behaviour 'underground' so as to avoid being criticized, rather than keeping focused on the primary goal of eliminating sexism.

Clearly a new analysis and programme of activity are needed.

GIVING UP CONTROL

I believe that the crucial issue in men's relationship with women and in working to eliminate sexism is control. Institutional sexism hands control to men as a group. While there are many men, especially in groups that suffer a double oppression, such as black men, who have precious little economic or social control as individuals, men as a group tend to be brought up to believe that women are inferior and sexism does put men into a dominant position, whether they desire it or not.

Therefore, the next step for men in learning how to treat women well and in eliminating sexism is to explore what it would mean to give up control. Some men may well think this is peculiar, since they often feel that, in practice, they are already controlled by women. Diane Balser[1], an international women's leader, belives that this is because most young people are primarily brought up by their mothers. As a result, some men may confuse the negative feelings they had about the 'adultism' in that mother/son relationship with current relationships with women as an adult. As I have said, however, in reality, at the institutional level, men are now and have always been predominant.

In my experience, giving up control is extremely difficult for men because being in control creates an illusion of security and predictability, while deciding to give up control is a frightening and humiliating step to take. 'Real men' are brought up with the expectation that they will be in control at every level, and if that control is given or taken away, feelings of insecurity that do not normally have to be faced will surface.

Men are brought up to exercise control in relation to women at three levels of their lives:

O   The control of institutions;
O   The control of personal relationships;
O   The control of feelings.

Each level will need to be challenged in a specific way in order to contradict the traditional patterns of behaviour involved.

Giving up institutional control

As argued in Chapter 5, all oppressions operate primarily at the institutional level where they become operationalized as a mixture of policy and practice – that is, the very systems, rules and regulations of the institution itself are designed to install and maintain the oppression and have become self-perpetuating. A good example of such a policy in relation to women as leaders has been the refusal until recently to allow women to become priests in some of the Christian churches.

These are the objective conditions of the oppression – the systematic denial of access, the poor wages or working conditions, and the inequality of opportunity for advancement, promotion or training. For example, as stated in Chapter 6, only about 3 per cent of top managers in British industry are women, and where women are promoted they are still mainly ghettoized into traditional 'feminine' roles such as personnel or training. Most women workers are part-time, on poor pay and have dreadful working conditions. They rarely have a union to represent them and end up having to take whatever work they can get because they need the money.

In an interview with Rosie Brennan as part of a project she was undertaking to prepare her book, *Equal Opportunities Practice in Seven Local Authorities*,[2] a woman responsible for leading equal opportunities initiatives in one authority said: 'There are a number of men who say they are really committed to equal opportunities in this organization, but when it comes to standing down so as to back a woman to get the job, I've never known one do it!'

This is the challenge – to decide to really support women's progress and advancement into institutional leadership. This means stepping aside when appropriate, developing a strategy in every situation to enable women fully to take charge, and to look for every opportunity to encourage and back women into leadership.

DECIDING TO SUPPORT WOMEN'S ADVANCEMENT

Men can experiment with a decision to put women's progress at the centre of their leadership by making and implementing the following decision:

'I decide to encourage, support and assist every woman I currently know and every woman I have yet to meet to advance into full leadership, regardless of how humiliating or terrifying it may leave me feeling.'

Then add the name of a specific woman into the decision, for example a colleague or a subordinate at work, to make it more particular to one's own situation.

Giving up control of relationships

The effect of sexism is to create a tacit expectation and agreement that men know more than women, and will act as the 'boss' even in an ordinary peer relationship. This is communicated most strongly to young men within the traditional family situation where the father may act in a strong and confident manner and is the disciplinarian, while the mother behaves as though she is of secondary importance. In reality, however, the mother often makes the decisions and holds the family together.

On the other hand, the way in which women are brought up to internalize sexism, as described in Chapter 6, means that women will often go to any lengths to mould themselves, their expectations and their behaviour into a 'shape' which they think men will approve of. I believe men have no idea of the extent to which women are prepared to subjugate their own desires and needs in order to be acceptable because of the effects of internalized sexism.

This produces a situation where it is difficult for many women to know what they really want for themselves. At this point, as I described in Chapter 7, women are challenged to 'settle for nothing less than absolutely everything' in thinking about and pursuing what makes sense for them in their own lives and in their leadership.

In these circumstances in particular, men as leaders can play a crucial role by learning to ask women what it is they want and then listening with complete respect. While doing this, men need to be completely patient and do what they are told, no matter how irritated or frustrated they may feel. Taking this step, like all the others, is extremely scary for both men and women but it is essential if we are to make progress.

ASKING WOMEN WHAT THEY WANT

The first step in giving up control is for men to ask women what they want for themselves and from men in every situation as it arises, rather than thinking on woman's behalf about what they should do or making assumptions about what women might need.

In practice, the way that internalized sexism affects an individual woman may well mean she is not able to answer immediately, but this is fine. It does not mean that the man has nothing to do; it means that he should wait and keep on asking.

Men need to listen with complete respect and strive for an attitude of complete delight in whatever they are told! In my experience, men will sometimes experiment with this action while actually resenting it beneath the surface. They may ask women what they want but not really want to hear the response, thus increasing women's mistrust rather than improving the situation. It is therefore very important that men monitor their true feelings and take care to communicate with integrity. They may need to spend more time obtaining help from someone else in order to deal with their feelings before they are able to ask women what they want and mean it.

Giving up control of feelings

Chapter 8 described the way that the systematic interference with the inherent human ability to feel and discharge, and its replacement with a heavy expectation of remaining thinking, fearless and aloof under any circumstances, is a central component of men's oppression. This is then internalized by men into the denial, repression of feelings and the pretence that they have no problems. In men's relationships with women this causes difficulties because men are so strongly 'programmed' to be brave, to 'put women first' and to be the protector.

Among men who have been addressing these issues for some time, there is, on occasion, a sophisticated version of the same pattern. For example, the man may well be feeling badly and needing to talk about his difficulties but instead moves into the role of sensitive listener, getting the woman to talk about her problems instead. Under these circumstances, the man has stayed in control of the relationship and in control of his feelings. Again, it is therefore essential that men monitor their motivation and communicate with integrity. Tackling pretence is a crucial part of making these changes effective.

In an organizational setting, the expectation that men will control their feelings is a major determinant of organizational culture, affecting men and women as leaders alike. For men as leaders, the possibility that women colleagues will 'break down' is particularly fearful and places huge pressures on women not to show weakness or admit to having difficulties.

This emotional self-control that men place upon themselves and the oppressive expectation that they then place on women has to be ended, and replaced with a new practice of thinking about the situation and, where appropriate, choosing to be vulnerable.

CHOOSING TO BE VULNERABLE

Men can experiment with a decision to be vulnerable and give up all pretence, making sure that as leaders they create time to review their own struggles and difficulties in their leadership. This can be supported by making the following decision and then considering its implications:

'I decide that I will be completely and utterly vulnerable, that I will feel absolutely everything that there is to feel, regardless of how humiliating or frightening it may be.'

This works very well in contradicting the old pattern of the stiff upper lip and releases men to play a human part in their interactions with women.

These, then, are the key steps that men need to take if they are to succeed in the goal of creating a new men's leadership and of eliminating sexism from the workplace.

REFERENCES

1.   *Women – Their Present Situation in the World*, Diane Balser (Rational Island Press, 1986).
2.   *Equal Opportunities in Seven Local Authorities*, by Rosemary Brennan (Local Government Management Board, 1989).

PART III
BUILDING AN INCLUSIVE ORGANIZATION

❖

The most important challenge facing us if we are to build successful and sustainable organizations is to shift our focus towards putting people at the centre of everything we do. This means finding ways of involving people – whether they are employed in the organization or are its customers – in contributing their thinking and their energy. The critical commitment is to ensure that anyone who is in any way connected with a common enterprise feels included and is delighted with their contact.

The main obstacle to achieving this goal is oppression. In Chapter 5, I postulated that the chief effect of oppression is to divide people and set them against one another on the basis of their membership of different groups. This leads to the creation of organizations which do not value the contribution that employees can make to their functioning, particularly from those groups of people which suffer institutionalized discrimination and are therefore excluded from the central processes of the organization. In addition, it leads to the creation of products or services which exclude some potential customers from their use because these people are regarded as unimportant or unprofitable.

THE PHENOMENON OF EXCLUSION

Exclusion is at the heart of oppression. It is the visible evidence that oppression is at work. Members of the dominant group always have what they regard as good reasons to justify why they should be included while others are not. For the people who are excluded it is an experience that is both painful and alienating.

Such practices are rooted in the underlying ideology of traditional leadership. The assumptions of superiority and power create a situation where some people are left out. We can see this most clearly dramatized in the way that people with disabilities are treated. So many assumptions and prejudices about the desires and abilities of disabled people are made without reference to the people themselves, and as a result they are ignored as customers and marginalized into particular low status occupations as employees.

This still tends to be true about women as a group and about some men on the basis of class or race. People in these groups are not regarded as important and are therefore excluded from the thinking of the most senior leaders. The challenge is to build an inclusive organization.

BUILDING AN INCLUSIVE ORGANIZATION

This requires a fundamental change in our awareness and consciousness. We need to begin to comprehend the profound interdependence that we have with one another. Our long-term survival will depend on our willingness to embrace the importance of cooperation and win–win rather than competition and win–lose. This means thinking and acting at all times so as to enhance and add to the quality of the lives of everyone rather than to the short-term interests of particular groups or individual representatives of those groups.

For this to happen we must understand that leadership is the central unifying and focusing process of the organization. In the hands of the formal leader is the responsibility for systematically reaching to include everyone in the organization in every process by developing good policies and a practice that is aimed at building an inclusive organization.

Developing policies and a practice that will lead to equality of opportunity are central to this process.

EQUALITY OF OPPORTUNITY

Working towards equality means eliminating institutional discrimination and personal prejudice towards people using the excuse of their gender, race, disability or any aspect of their identity not relevant to their working lives.

Working towards equal opportunities makes a contribution to the enterprise and to each and every person involved in it by:

O   Releasing the vast and untapped potential of the majority of people in the organization, who have been traditionally under-valued and under-utilized through the operation of discrimination and prejudice.

O   Dismantling the roles of oppressor and oppressed which demean everyone by being caught up in an inhuman process.

TAKING POSITIVE ACTION

During the past ten years, many organizations have committed themselves to improving equality of opportunity and there are now many policy statements and declarations in existence. However, merely claiming to treat all people equally is not sufficient because it ignores the undoubted differences in people's starting points that result from past discrimination. Positive action is necessary to undo the effects of past mistreatment on people who have been subjected to discrimination and prejudice. In addition, work is necessary with people in formal leadership positions to help them to review and eliminate the impact of any prejudicial attitudes that they hold in order to stop further mistreatment at its source.

It is important to differentiate between positive discrimination and positive action. Positive discrimination takes place where members of a particular group are given jobs simply because their group has been identified as suffering discrimination. Quotas are an example of positive discrimination since they state that a certain number of people from a particular group must be taken on in order to achieve a certain level of representation. The affirmative action legislation in the United States allows organizations to discriminate positively in favour of the members of identified groups, although these laws are now under considerable attack.

Positive discrimination does not seem to work well. To begin with it tends to leave both the person targeted and those who have not been targeted feeling badly. The person who got the job due to their membership of an oppressed group is often left feeling that the job was undeserved and they only got it because of the policy. The people who did not get the job are left feeling that the person who did is not really good enough for it and only got it because of membership of the oppressed group, and any apparent failure on the successful candidate's part usually unleashes huge attacks.

This antagonism towards the individual beneficiaries of the policy often turns into a general backlash against the policy and the group concerned, because everyone begins to feel that people do not get jobs on merit but because of favours.

Positive action does not allow positive discrimination in favour of the members of particular groups, but recognizes the impact of discrimination on people's starting points. It encourages action to enable the members of groups that suffer oppression to improve the foundations on which they stand. For example, we might offer special training opportunities to women who have historically been denied access to training.

Most progressive organizations now have positive action programmes to help the members of groups that are identified as facing discrimination to develop and improve. A typical example, aimed at overcoming the disadvantages black people face in one local government organization, is a programme called 'Racing Ahead' which includes training aimed at increasing confidence and skills to handle people at the same level and senior colleagues.

One of the most successful programmes aimed at women in the United Kingdom is the 'Woman's Development Course' at the Civil Service College. This has been running for more than 15 years and has given a large number of women the opportunity to review their approach and to increase their self-confidence and assertiveness, and then to develop a career plan.

All of these programmes, however, are dependent on the commitment and understanding of top management, and, in my experience, the changes in attitude needed are so profound that most people take a year or two to really implement the change.

However, while the concept of the inclusive organization includes all of these practices, it reaches beyond them to ensure that everyone is fully included. In particular, it is important to realize the importance of embracing white able-bodied men. While, historically, they have had many privileges, I am proposing that we take into account that men are oppressed, though not by women or children, and work to ensure that the organization is a good place for them.

Part III outlines the processes, attitudes and skills that need to be developed in order to build an inclusive organization. Chapter 10, 'A New System of Leadership', describes the five components of a new system of leadership that can be integrated into any positive action strategy to ensure that everyone is included.

Chapter 11, 'The Attributes of a Leader', introduces the five attributes needed for supporting the new system of leadership. Chapter 12, 'Developing New Skills', lays out the five most important skills required for maintaining the new system of leadership.

Chapter 13, 'Tools and Formats', describes my approach to coaching and counselling and an approach to leadership development I call the 'Leadership Development Meeting'.

Chapter 14, 'A Programme for Change', describes a proposed strategy for developing an inclusive organization.

The final chapter, 'Training for Women and Men' describes the basic principles and structure for leadership and gender awareness training for women and men.

10

A NEW SYSTEM OF LEADERSHIP

Building an inclusive organization calls for outstanding leadership effort at every level of the enterprise over a sustained period. Leadership is the fundamental integrating process that puts people at the centre of the organization and without it there can be no progress. The challenge is to enable everyone to contribute their full intelligence, creativity and initiative.

We need a new system of leadership designed to ensure that people, and particularly people who have been traditionally excluded, are fully included in the process of managing and improving how the organization works. For example, I think it is apparent that bringing women fully into the organization will liberate a very special energy and way of looking at the world, but making it happen will require that people in formal leadership positions decide to take positive action to achieve it.

We must therefore adopt an approach that will increase the opportunities for people to contribute, but in addition we must invest in equipping the people we want to contribute to be able to do so effectively. Without a positive action strategy, institutional discrimination and prejudice will act to inhibit all change in the hoped for direction.

I believe that the process for achieving this comprises five basic steps, each one leading to the next and making in total a new system of leadership. The steps are illustrated in Figure 10.1.

In practice, it sometimes makes sense to begin with an activity aimed at increasing our understanding of the whole situation rather than beginning with vision. The choice will ideally depend on the level of security felt by the person or group undertaking the work. If a person has a low level of security, starting with the process of developing a vision will increase the sense of security, making the rest of the work go well. Where a person has high security, beginning with information about the present situation may be best, because it increases people's dissatisfaction with the present situation and therefore increases openness to learning.

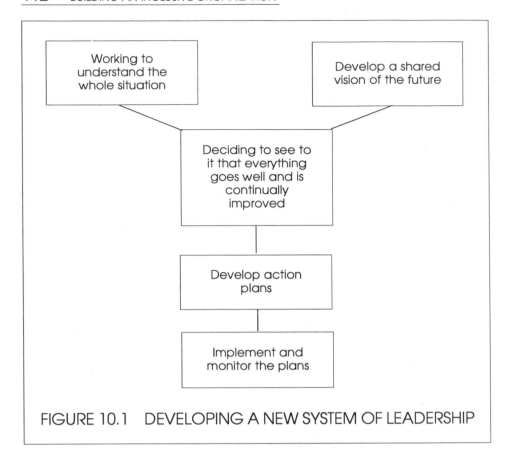

FIGURE 10.1   DEVELOPING A NEW SYSTEM OF LEADERSHIP

DEVELOPING A SHARED VISION

As the song from the show *South Pacific* says – 'You gotta have a dream! If you don't have a dream, how you gonna have a dream come true?'. Having a dream and working to achieve it is an important part of being in charge of one's own life. Turning that dream into a working vision of the future, encouraging other people to do the same and then building a shared vision are among the most powerful processes I know for building an inclusive organization.

First, dreams help provide us with a guiding direction which is good to remember when we face discouragement. Building an inclusive organization is a difficult road with many setbacks and disappointments. A vision is a source of inspiration and therefore a great contradiction to the feelings of failure and powerlessness that people are bound to experience. Second, when we involve as many people as possible in developing a shared vision, it provides a unifying force for collaboration and action. Third, if we are to continually improve the performance of the organization as a system, we must be clear about its aim – as the aphorism says, 'when you are up to your arse in alligators it is sometimes difficult to remember that you came here to drain the swamp'! Developing a vision of the future leads us towards a clear definition of the aim of the enterprise.

It is therefore essential that people at every level, develop a clear vision of where they are aiming to be, communicate that vision widely and do not abandon it, even if they have to change their strategy for achieving it to meet changing circumstances as they proceed.

DEVELOPING A VISION

Exercise 10.1   Developing a vision

To develop your own vision, ask yourself the question: 'How would things be around here (in my workplace, family, community etc.) if they were meeting my most deeply held values and beliefs?'.

Write down your replies as they come into your head and then put them into some kind of order that helps them to make sense. This can then become your vision of the future.

When you are thinking about how you would like your vision to be, it is important to allow yourself to be idealistic. In the planning stage, we need to come up with a thoroughly realistic plan that takes full account of the situation in the external environment, within the organization itself and for the individuals who work in it, but our vision needs to be based on what we value and believe is most important if it is to have real meaning for us.

HELPING OTHER PEOPLE TO DEVELOP THEIR VISION

Learning how to help other people develop their own vision is an important part of the new leadership. The process of developing a vision works best if someone else is paying us attention, asking us the question 'How would things be if they were meeting your most deeply held values and beliefs?', encouraging us to express our best thinking and making notes on what we say so that we can elaborate the ideas later. The other person can encourage us to think big and give us plenty of appreciation for our ideas as we reach for our dreams.

As we provide this help to other people, we may find that women and men have different strengths and difficulties in doing it successfully. Many women have been brought up with the expectation that they will fulfil their dreams primarily through other people, namely men and children. At first, this can make it difficult for them to put themselves at the centre of the process and to think about what they value and believe is important, but it is very important that they reclaim and build on their own dreams of how things could and should be for them and for everyone else. This implies lots of appreciation for every thought, no matter how big or small, and plenty of encouragement to think bigger.

For example, I worked with a female management development adviser in local government who suffered from a kind of myopia when it came to developing her vision. She was unable to think beyond small aspirations for herself or for her organization. In working with her, it was essential that her colleagues and I were patient and encouraging while she struggled to get her thinking out, but at the same time, being firmly supportive about her ability to think bigger still.

For men, the pull is to see things solely in terms of materialistic achievement and task-orientation. In a way, this leaves them better able to think big and yet in danger of leaving themselves as a person and their relationships with other people out of the picture. It can be useful when helping men to develop their vision to remind them to put themselves and their deepest human needs right at the centre of the process, and go on from there to consider how to embrace every other person fully as an integral part of their vision.

WORKING TOGETHER ON A VISION

Working together to develop a shared vision is the most exciting step in building an inclusive organization. It can be an empowering and trust-building activity especially if people are encouraged to develop their own vision first. As Peter Senge writes:

> Shared visions emerge from personal visions, this is how the organization fosters personal commitment. Only your own vision motivates you because it is about your own set of values, concerns and aspirations. This is why genuine caring about a shared vision is rooted in personal visions. This simple truth is lost on many leaders, who decide that their organizations must develop vision by tomorrow.[1]

Some people become concerned about the prospect of different people having very different visions and these different visions then causing conflict. My experience is that this is rarely the case. For example, I worked over several years with management and trade union officials in a quarry in the Peak District of England, and when I asked each group to develop its own vision and then share it with the other group there was much agreement between them. In most situations, people's inherent humanness comes through and as a consequence, most people want very similar things. Where there were differences among people in the quarry, these added new dimensions and colour and people often said 'Yes, I hadn't thought of that, but I think it is a good idea'. There is usually sufficient common ground on which to proceed and any remaining differences can be resolved later.

THE CONCEPT OF 'MINIMUM AGREEMENT'

Where there are differences that seem irreconcilable, I always find it helpful to look for areas of agreement rather than disagreement. I was once working in a large insurance company with a training manager and his team and there appeared to be much disagreement about their vision of the future. I invited them to look for the areas of 'minimum agreement' where everybody could say

'Yes!' as the basis for moving things forward and this unblocked what had seemed like insurmountable obstacles.

INVOLVING THE WHOLE ORGANIZATION

It is possible to take positive action to involve everybody in the organization in developing a vision of the future. Beginning at the top, we can develop a strategy that cascades the vision to senior and middle managers and then down to all staff. In a project with a glass manufacturing company, I encouraged the top team to develop a 'charter for the future' which they then invited senior management teams to discuss in a meeting. These teams were then asked to develop their own charter and then pass this back to the top team. Over a period of five years it was possible to take this process right down through the organization.

In an increasing number of organizations, large groups of people have been brought together for an 'alignment meeting'. A workshop is designed which enables people to think collectively about the present situation and deepen their understanding of what is happening. Top managers then present their vision and everyone else is then encouraged to think about their own. These may then be written up on flip-charts and presented in small groups, and similarities and differences explored. Finally, the flip-charts are displayed around the room and people of all levels mixed together to discuss and strive for overall agreement.

WORKING TO UNDERSTAND THE WHOLE SITUATION

When I look at much of the leadership in the world, it is apparent that people continually make the decision to see to it that everything goes well, but frequently their decisions are based on an inadequate understanding of the whole situation. This can lead to dangerous and harmful consequences for the people involved in the situation. We see this all too often in politics, where politicians present poorly thought out proposals based on an inadequate study of the situation and then insist on implementing the proposals regardless of any emerging evidence that contradicts the course of action they are taking. Too often our decisions are based on a simple linear analysis, missing out the huge complexity of interconnected processes that make up a system.

As long ago as 1972, Geoffrey Vickers wrote:

> The most striking feature of human beings, when compared with other animals, is not their ingenuity in doing – that 'goal-seeking' of which we have heard too much – but their capacity for knowing where they are. They can represent to themselves their contexts – all those manifold relations with the world around them which they pursue and on which they rely and which help to define their meaning to themselves and others.[2]

Reaching to 'represent to ourselves our contexts' is a crucial part of any new leadership initiative. It is about increasing our appreciation of the total system in which our activities are taking place rather than making do with a narrow and limited view.

We have to develop a view of our context based upon an understanding of the complexity of interrelationships rather than looking for linear causalities. This systems-orientated approach has become increasingly important as the rate of change and level of ambiguity have increased. We must learn to resist simple solutions, but instead look towards a profound understanding of our total environment.

I call this process 'Working to understand the whole situation'. This is the first half of the definition of leadership introduced in Chapter 2 and it is an essential part of the foundations of an inclusive organization. It assumes that any one of us has only a small part of the information, perspective, experience, insight and thinking needed to make sense of any given situation, and that we need to reach out to others to understand fully what is going on. In this sense, I believe that we are all 'apprentices' who are engaged in a lifetime process of learning, and as we learn we begin to see that there is even more to learn. Learning is a joyous and delightful activity as we rediscover and release that aspect of our inherent nature.

UNDERSTANDING THE ISSUES SURROUNDING INCLUSION

When we have as a goal the building of an inclusive organization, there are particular issues and concerns that we need to appreciate fully. We must understand how discrimination and prejudice are operating in our organization, how people have internalized the oppression and what the costs are to the people who are in the role of discriminator.

In proposing this, I do not intend to imply that we will ever achieve a complete understanding because, in practice, this will be neither possible nor necessary. For example, it is not possible for a man to completely comprehend the situation that a woman might face because he will not have had the opportunity of experiencing things a woman has experienced. However, if he can begin to see the limitations of his understanding and appreciate fully that it is essential to include women in every activity because they have knowledge and experience that he does not have, he will have made enormous strides in being effective as a leader.

In thinking about who to ask when we wish to learn more, I propose that we reach in particular for the views of people who would generally not be heard in the organization, whoever they are. It is all too easy to listen to the women who have reached the senior levels (although, in practice, I think they are rarely given a proper hearing), but it is even more valuable to ask women who are in junior positions how they experience the organization. In a project I undertook in a government research department, the director scheduled a series of meetings on Friday afternoons open to women from all levels to come to talk with him. He was staggered to hear women talk of constant discourtesy and disrespect from their male colleagues and discovered a significant case of sexual harassment that had been going on for some time but which no one had felt able to speak up about before.

The key skill in working to understand the whole situation is learning how to ask interesting questions and then listening with complete respect and I examine this in more detail in Chapter 12.

DECIDING TO SEE TO IT THAT EVERYTHING GOES WELL

Based on a growing understanding of the whole situation we can decide to see to it that absolutely everything in it goes well without limit or reservation. This is the second half of the definition of leadership proposed in Chapter 2 and the third step in the new system of leadership. Having developed a vision of the future it is then crucial to decide to see to it that it is achieved. More than that, it is essential that we make the decision about the whole situation, whether it is one that we typically think of as being within our own domain or not.

This decision is the most powerful contradiction to powerlessness that I know. It means deciding to take complete charge, thinking well about what needs to be done, taking action to do it and then reviewing the action to see if it has worked, and replanning where necessary.

The key word here is 'deciding' and we must decide not just once but repeatedly. Chronic patterns have an unfortunate habit of returning to haunt us just when we think we have them beaten, and powerlessness is a very entrenched pattern in almost all human beings. We will need repeatedly to decide if we are to claim our full power to put things right.

We are engaged in a process of discovering and learning how to use our 'will' to make things happen. There will be times when we 'forget', or allow discouragement to creep in, or feel that we have taken on too much and we need to bring our will to bear to carry us through. We need not be hard on ourselves if we 'go off the job' occasionally. However, once we notice that this has happened, we need to redecide and get on with the job.

Another crucial word here is 'everything'. This means that we do not walk past any issue needing to be addressed, even if, at an initial glance, it looks as though it has nothing to do with us. People have an extraordinary and under-used ability to think about many different issues, take appropriate responsibility for them and then strategize how best to ensure that things go well. So, for example, we can bring any concern that we have to the attention of other people and ask them to join us in doing something about it rather than doing it alone.

Another aspect of this step is to define clearly what we mean by 'everything going well'. Different people may value different things, and these values will guide their action. In my experience, it is helpful to base our leadership on a sound theoretical base. We can then develop policies and practices based upon that theory. In building an inclusive organization, I have found the theory and practice put forward in this book to be an excellent basis for deciding what it means to see to it that 'everything goes well' in any given situation. There is no inherent conflict between human beings engaged in rational activities, so 'going well' must include that there is no oppression or exploitation of anyone in the situation.

Again, the challenges for women and for men are somewhat different in implementing this action because of the effects of gender conditioning. Many women already operate from this viewpoint in some form or other because of the societal expectation that they will take care of everything. Our task is therefore to assist women to notice that they do this already and to encourage them to be more 'up front' about it, rather than doing it 'behind the scenes' as they might have done traditionally.

For men, taken out of context the action could be misconstrued as encouraging a new attempt to control everything based on the assumption that they know best. The necessary antidote to what might appear to be arrogance is to strive for an understanding that one cannot see to it that everything goes well effectively without having a deep understanding of the whole situation, and this is done primarily by listening to other people. This often means that men will concentrate on supporting other people's leadership by encouraging them to have the major influence on the decision as to the best way to proceed – particularly, for example, in the case of women's leadership.

MAKING DETAILED PLANS OF ACTION

The next step is to develop detailed actions plans. I like to use an approach that starts with thinking about one's vision of the future and, working backwards through time, ends up with the specific actions that need to be taken tomorrow.

The process requires the following steps:

O   To develop a clear vision of how you would like things to be by using the approach described above in Exercise 10.1. Write your vision down.

O   To make a best guess about how long it will take to achieve the vision, based upon your experience and your best thinking.

You are now ready to begin the detailed goal setting needed to be undertaken if you are to achieve your vision by the date you have estimated. You will work backwards, halving the period at each step.

O   If you estimated, say, ten years to achieve your vision, then choose five years, and then ask the question, 'What would I need to do within the next five years if I am to achieve my vision in ten years' time?' Write down your answer.

O   Halve the period again, and ask the same question, but for the new period – 'What would I need to do within the next two years if I am to achieve my goals for the first five years?' Write this down.

O   Halve the period again and again, each time writing down your thinking, until you get to, say, one week, and then ask, 'What will I need to have done by this time tomorrow, if I am to achieve my goals for the end of the next week?'

This seems to work very effectively in helping people to have a clear vision of where they are going and then providing concrete goals for achieving it.

ACTION PLANNING IN A WORK GROUP

This process can be used to great effect with teams of people who work together. Developing plans as a group is most unifying and helps to build people's cooperation when it comes to implementation. It is most powerful if each member of the team plans what they will do individually in the presence of the others. This increases the probability of liberating individual initiative. A good way of doing this is the leadership development meeting which is described in Chapter 13.

IMPLEMENT THE ACTION PLAN AND REVIEW PERFORMANCE

It is crucial that we go ahead and implement what we have planned. Sound thinking, clear viewpoints, well worked out strategies are all necessary but they count for nothing without action. In my experience, many people understand the need for new and better leadership, have got to the point of saying 'Yes' but have then hesitated, thinking 'But what can I do?'

To think about something and not act on that thinking undermines one's own intelligence, reduces self-esteem and feeds powerlessness. In many cases it is better to do something (based on our best thinking) and review how it goes, than do nothing. We can always adjust what we do if it is not fully effective, because we have that special human quality of intelligence, the ability to come up with a fresh, new and appropriate response to any new situation. We can learn as we take action.

REFERENCES

1.   *The Fifth Discipline*, Peter Senge (Century Business, 1990).
2.   *Freedom in a Rocking Boat*, Geoffrey Vickers (Penguin Books, 1972).

11
THE ATTRIBUTES OF A LEADER

To build an inclusive organization is one of the most demanding challenges that any individual has ever faced. The new system of leadership offers a step-by-step process towards a positive action approach, but if we are to implement it successfully we need to engage in an intensive review of our underlying attitudes towards ourselves and others. The effects of individual hurts and oppression tend to limit the ability of most of us to be able to begin, and then in turn sustain a long-term commitment to this vision in the face of a pressing social and economic environment. We all need to increase our understanding of our own limitations and work systematically to overcome them with the support of others, including the people at the top.

I have worked with many chief executives and senior managers, all with significant strengths and abilities and thoroughly committed to improving the performance of their organizations, but, almost without exception, they have been characterized by an obsession with quick results. This is both a positive attribute and a weakness. It keeps them going and it ensures that things get done, but the new leadership requires people to focus at least as much on the process in order to ensure that everyone is included and that the way the work is done is continually improved. Unfortunately, the focus on results affects people right down through the enterprise creating the culture of traditional leadership. It takes hard work to turn from that approach, putting people at the centre of the organization, adopting the new system of leadership, and building an inclusive organization.

We need to begin work on a personal development programme aimed at strengthening our abilities across a number of personal characteristics or traits. Of the many possibilities, I have identified five characteristics that I regard as central to success in building an inclusive organization and I term these the Five Key Attributes of a New Leadership. They provide the foundations on which the five steps of the new system of leadership can then be built and are the following:

O   Taking our leadership completely seriously.
O   Developing high self-esteem.
O   Making close, dependable relationships the basis of everything we do.
· O   Becoming a leader of leaders.
O   Taking positive initiatives instead of complaining and blaming.

TAKING OUR LEADERSHIP COMPLETELY SERIOUSLY

We need to decide to take ourselves, our ability to contribute to the organizations in which we work and our importance as leaders completely seriously, regardless of the position that we are in. Many of us do not appreciate our significance in the world, not only in our workplace but also to our families, our friends and our neighbours. A big hurt for all of us growing up and as workers in organizations is to be told that we are not important and that taking ourselves seriously is arrogant and self-centred. In reality, however, who better to influence events? Who better to lead other people and make a big contribution to improving everything? I do not mean this in any traditional sense of pompous, status-conscious significance, but rather seeing ourselves as important as human beings having intelligence, creativity, goodness and human power, capable of achieving anything we put our minds to.

Women in particular need to develop this attribute as a contradiction to the invisibility which has for so long been a consequence of sexism and women's internalized oppression. The gender conditioning which encourages young women to see themselves primarily as 'carers' rather than as 'achievers' leaves many adult women prepared to settle for less than they are really capable of. We must encourage all women to understand their true importance in the world and constantly emphasize that their way of doing things, while it may be different from the way many men behave, is not only excellent but essential.

There are also many men who have settled for timidity and compliance as a consequence of men's oppression and its internalization. Taking oneself seriously is an excellent contradiction for anyone who feels powerless or in any way a 'victim' of the situation in which they find themselves.

It does not have to be a serious business. It can be great fun to notice one's ideas, influence and impact and the ripples created. We are all part of a huge network of thoughts and actions in an 'ecological' process of change. That is, 'ecological' in the sense of being part of a large system where changes in one segment can have knock-on effects throughout the whole which we may not initially expect or fully appreciate.

Encouraging other people to take themselves seriously is a fundamental part of building an inclusive organization. We are working to create an environment where everyone is valued in their own right and where they are encouraged to contribute. This will only be successful if people work at taking themselves seriously, accepting their value and deciding to contribute.

DEVELOPING HIGH SELF-ESTEEM

Genuine self-esteem is present when we are pleased with ourselves whatever other people feel or say. When we experience it, we could say that we are in touch with our inherent human nature. Consequently, we value ourselves, respecting and trusting our own thinking and are thoroughly delighted with the things we do. Self-esteem underpins the decision to take ourselves seriously.

Self-esteem is not to be confused with arrogance, smugness or pretence, which are products of low self-esteem. It shows most in the relationship we have with ourselves once we have given up criticizing ourselves, giving ourselves a hard time in situations where we have done our best, or allowed ourselves to be racked with guilt about things we have done wrong.

If we are to be successful in seeing through the decision to see to it that everything goes well, we need to feel good about ourselves and have real self-confidence; we need to work at contradicting the accumulation of invalidation and 'put downs' that distort and restrict our ability to function well in every part of our lives, as described in Chapters 4 and 5.

This is an area of particular vulnerability for women. Just imagine growing up in a culture which says in many different ways that people like you are never successful, and in order to be successful you need to be a member of this other group. Institutionalized sexism is so much built into the fabric of this society, and, while there are women who are not badly damaged by it, it has a major impact on all women's lives.

In reality, many men also suffer with low self-esteem. Remember that men are an oppressed group too, that every man is taught that there is a clear specification for how to behave as a 'real man', and that no man comes up to scratch. However, sexism does give many men some semblance of value and this can give them the basis for high self-esteem. Do not confuse this with the urge to prove oneself or the arrogance that some men take on which is, in fact, based on low self-esteem.

A CHANGE OF VIEWPOINT IS NEEDED

A great influence of mine, Harvey Jackins, has written:

> Every human being has at every moment of the past, when the entire situation is taken into account, done the very best that he or she could do, and so deserves neither blame nor reproach from anyone, including themselves.
> This in particular is true of you![1]

This one statement captures the essence of my message.

However, since throughout our lives we have all been subjected to a vast amount of criticism, blame and attack, most of us suffer a deficit in our self-esteem account which is not of our own making. The best contradiction or antidote to this deficit is to make the decision to remember that we are completely good, that we have done the very best we can, given the circumstances, and that we do not deserve blame or reproach from anyone.

Therefore, encouraging women to like and appreciate themselves, to notice their effectiveness and the importance of their contribution, and to give up all self-criticism is essential. The work is very similar for men – to claim one's goodness as a man, to like oneself just as one is and to decide that there is nothing that needs to be proved.

MAKING THE DECISION TO REMEMBER THAT WE ARE GOOD

I will remember I am good and that I have always done the very best I could when the whole situation is taken into account. I do not need to take a negative view of myself or to puff up my importance. I am learning how to do things better all of the time and I will improve. In the meantime, I am enough as I am!

We can practise the skills of self-appreciation and being appreciated by others and I will describe in detail how to this in Chapter 12.

MAKE CLOSE, DEPENDABLE RELATIONSHIPS THE BASIS OF EVERYTHING WE DO

Strategies and plans, policies and procedures, guidelines and standards are all extremely useful in organizing joint endeavour, but in a time of constant and turbulent change we need something more. Amid all this change what can we build that will provide security and hope?

I believe our best chance is in our relationships with other people, particularly if we are able to build close, dependable relationships which transcend fashions and temporary dramas. None of the leadership steps will work without close, dependable relationships with many people in all parts of the enterprise – particularly people different from ourselves.

This has many benefits. One is to combat the divisiveness which the oppressive system generates and which makes it difficult for people to cooperate effectively to change things. Another is that when unforeseen difficulties arise we will have allies with whom to work to solve problems and make new plans. Yet another is that we will break down the isolation that many of us struggle with as the result of past mistreatment. It is particularly important for people taking leadership to overcome the potential for isolation that so often accompanies the formal position because this has been such a central and defeating aspect of traditional leadership.

Building close, dependable relationships means acting with integrity, giving up all manipulation, and paying attention to others rather than to ourselves – people will then feel respected and able to trust us with their futures.

This is an area where women are traditionally very strong. Their training for 'caring' encourages women to do what they have to do through relationships with other people rather than through trying to push ahead with the task as though other people do not exist. However, this approach is still not highly valued in most traditional organizations and so women need to be encouraged to trust their own thinking and approach rather than adopting a 'masculine' way of doing things.

For many men, however, it is perhaps the most difficult thing to do. Time spent building relationships often feels like an interference in the real work of achieving targets. Men need lots of support to understand and value the importance of this and plenty of encouragement to practise doing it.

BECOMING A CENTRE OF BENIGN INFLUENCE

When we build close, dependable relationships with other people across the organization as a whole we can begin to see ourselves as a centre of benign influence. This notion is rooted in an understanding that people live in a network of relationships. If we think well about a number of people and encourage them to think well about others, we can build a constituency of people who are supporting one another, sharing a common vision and working together to construct it; thus bringing a benign influence to bear. To be at the centre means being connected to many people who are themselves connected to many people so that our influence spreads rapidly and widely.

I return to the skills needed for building close, dependable relationships in Chapter 13.

BECOMING A LEADER OF LEADERS

Becoming a leader of leaders, rather than a leader of followers, follows naturally from the concept of becoming a centre of benign influence and is central to the notion of an inclusive organization. Given the importance of involving everyone in all aspects of managing the enterprise and the impossibility of doing everything ourselves anyway, encouraging people to see themselves as leaders in their own right is at the heart of this process.

This means treating everyone with complete respect, having high expectations of them, encouraging and appreciating their leadership, and giving them attention to deal with any difficulties when appropriate and preferably on a reciprocal basis. High expectations should not begin to feel like pressure on people, but rather come with a relaxed and confident assumption that they are natural leaders with all the inherent qualities needed. People only need to be reminded of this when they occasionally forget.

An important part of becoming a leader of leaders is to understand the importance of being open about one's own difficulties. Vulnerability is regarded as a symptom of weakness in traditional leadership, but if we want to include people and encourage their contribution they must be able to contribute to the effectiveness of those of us in formal leadership positions. This means asking for help and requesting feedback on how we are doing in our leadership. When undertaking supervision or appraisal, we can ask people's opinions about how we contribute to the difficulties and how we could improve the overall situation. This is sometimes called 'upwards appraisal'.

In a traditional leadership organization it can be more difficult to establish this kind of approach, so this can be handled by adopting the viewpoint of a leader among leaders but calling it 'delegation'. Most people understand and like the idea of delegation, but we can take it much further than that, moving the culture along as we go.

The other aspect of being a leader of leaders is to seek out and build relationships with other people who are taking leadership in areas related to but different from our own leadership. This provides excellent opportunities to learn, to understand more of the whole situation, to build allies across different issues, and to see our own significance in the wider scheme of things.

There are some situations where leaders need to work together as leaders, each with their own constituency or particular area. In these cases someone needs to take on the job of being a leader of leaders. This task requires all of the viewpoints and actions discussed here plus the ability to help people in their leadership and their development as leaders. A design for a meeting to do this is described in detail in Chapter 13.

Being a leader of leaders is another area in which women are already strong, but they need encouragement to lead more extensively. Men tend to have greater difficulties, being brought up to be more individualistic, self-centred and self-reliant. They will need to work hard to place supporting the development of other people over and above short-term results or looking good themselves.

TAKING POSITIVE INITIATIVES INSTEAD OF COMPLAINING OR BLAMING

Powerlessness is one of the biggest difficulties in building an inclusive organization. The history of traditional leadership sits like a heavy weight upon the shoulders of most people and they struggle enormously when asked to join with others in taking charge. So often in working with different parts of the Civil Service in the United Kingdom, senior managers told me that 'staff do not want more responsibility, they just want to do as little as possible and then complain about how they are managed'. Past mistreatment and internalized oppression leave people with a chronic feeling of powerlessness, which is the antithesis of leadership.

Symptoms of powerlessness include cynicism (which is really a kind of frozen disappointment), hopelessness, apathy, withdrawal and blaming others for the situation in which we find ourselves. These are all an indication of powerlessness because, when we criticize or complain about what someone else should be doing, we make them responsible for our difficulties. Effectively, we are saying that we have no ability to influence the situation, which is never true.

A particularly common example of powerlessness in organizations is to locate blame with people in formal leadership positions. Formal leaders have a great deal of power and influence over other people's lives, so it is easy to slip into blaming the leader if everything is not going well. It may be disguised as healthy debate, constructive criticism, or testing whether the leader is open-minded, but it is not helpful either to those criticizing or those criticized.

Such behaviour tends to be rooted in our experiences of people in authority positions, beginning with our parents, then with teachers and finally at work. Most of us have had bad experiences, and we often replay the situation towards people in formal leadership positions. Sometimes we are justified in feeling bad; a colleague, David Moscow, once said to me, 'Michael, you don't have a problem with people in authority, you just haven't worked for a decent authority figure yet'! However, there are many situations where we 'act out' being badly treated rather than taking complete charge of them ourselves.

TAKING POSITIVE INITIATIVES

To make progress in this area we have to begin by deciding to give up criticizing, blaming and attacking either ourselves or other people. This produces a better climate in which people can learn more effectively, and it helps us to shake off some of the powerlessness in which we get caught up when we behave in this way.

The next step is to take the initiative to see to it that everything goes well. Some years ago I wrote a slogan which I have found helpful ever since; namely, 'Every complaint is an action waiting to be taken'. I first 'invented' this insight in 1985 when training equal opportunities advisers in local government. They were locked into blaming their top managers for failing to implement the policies that the managers had themselves created. I encouraged the advisers to think about how they could take complete charge of the situation, develop an action plan and see it through no matter how long it took. I told them that 'every one of your complaints about other people or the system as a whole is an action waiting to be taken'. This viewpoint can help us to take charge and encourages us to work out how to help others.

Once we begin to convert complaints into action we have started to reclaim our personal powerfulness in the situation. Another viewpoint useful in pursuing this approach is that 'The past is determined but the future always offers freedom to choose'. Everything that has happened up until now has happened and there is nothing we can do about it. However, in the future, everything is up for grabs. We can decide to think and act in whatever way we like, whether it is sensible or not. Given that perspective, we are always free to start over again however things have gone before.

But the future is not just one single opportunity to decide how we want things to be. It is made up of countless new opportunities, each one arriving from over the hill one after the other and each one offering another fresh start. So, we do not need to become bogged down in feelings of failure.

From that upbeat viewpoint, it can be useful to think through a number of steps to convert a complaint into an action. First, we can appreciate ourselves for caring enough to see that something is wrong and needs to be put right. This, of course, is a part of taking ourselves seriously and improving our self-esteem.

Second, we can do some work on ourselves and our difficulty. We can identify the events that we do not like and what feelings are aroused. These feelings will be the same old bad feelings that often divert us when things get hard. We are then faced with a choice. We can decide to focus our attention on other people and the task in hand or we may need a hand from someone else to help us deal with the feelings of disappointment or outrage. The choice will depend on several factors: the opportunities available to deal effectively with our bad feelings about the situation, how much time we have, the level of risk involved, our likely success in being able to decide where to focus and keep our attention, and so on.

Once we have decided to do something other than complaining, blaming or attacking, we can strategize what we would do if we decided to take complete charge of the situation. When this is difficult, I find it helpful to imagine what someone I respect and admire might do. All these thoughts and ideas are useful indicators for what we actually need to do to take a positive initiative in the situation.

THE FIVE KEY ATTRIBUTES OF A LEADER

○   Taking our leadership completely seriously: Seeing our own significance as a human being, as a leader and as part of a network of leaders.

○   Developing high self-esteem: Developing the real self-confidence needed to see to it that everything goes well, by appreciating ourselves for what we have done well, and getting others to do the same, particularly in the places that we struggle the most.

○   Making close, dependable relationships the basis of everything we do: One of the best ways to win the energy and commitment of others and overcoming the isolation of leadership is by reaching for and building mutually supportive relationships with everyone. Become a centre of benign influence.

○   Becoming a leader of leaders: Treating everyone with complete respect as a potential leader, training and encouraging them and becoming a leader of leaders, not a leader of followers. Build close relationships with leaders in other spheres.

○   Taking positive initiatives instead of complaining or blaming: Reclaiming our personal powerfulness by giving up complaining or blaming ourselves or others. 'Every complaint is an action waiting to be taken'. Interrupting attacks on leaders. Giving up silent complaining. Plan how to take charge of the situation.

REFERENCES

1.   *Quotes*, Harvey Jackins (Rational Island Press, 1993).

12

DEVELOPING NEW SKILLS

❖

Effective leadership to build an inclusive organization requires the use of highly sophisticated personal skills designed to empower the people we work with to contribute and develop.

The basic assumption that guides my practice when working with people to develop these skills is that human beings are inherently intelligent, cooperative, zestful and powerful. In this book, I have argued that our ability to function effectively is damaged first by being hurt and then by the effects of being prohibited from engaging in the recovery and healing processes of discharge and evaluation. I have demonstrated that such hurts can be the result of an accident, contagion or oppression, and that hurts due to oppression are probably the most significant. I have postulated that it is a real hurt to our inherent human nature to take on the role of oppressor.

I proposed in Chapter 4, however, that we can recover from the effects of these hurts if there is a sufficient contradiction existing in the workplace and in our lives to counter the way that we feel about ourselves. But, in order to create this contradiction we must begin by assuming that we are free to choose our viewpoint on all things. A 'viewpoint' is any position or perspective that we adopt on a particular issue. For example, we can see a glass as half empty or we can see it as half full. The facts are the same but the viewpoint is different.

This approach is decisive because it means that, while we have been influenced by our experiences, we are also free to choose not to see ourselves as their victim. It means we have a position or policy to guide us when making judgements and taking action. A viewpoint can be a constant reminder which helps keep us on course when feelings arise and there is a danger of confusion in our thinking. However, viewpoints need not be rigid; it is necessary from time to time to reappraise our viewpoints, particularly as we learn more about the whole situation.

Mounting a contradiction comprises introducing just such a viewpoint – for example, 'People can improve!' While the hurts that people receive do place limits on their ability to function, we can also assume that people's inherent nature is still intact and that people retain the possibility of reclaiming their full, flexible intelligence, no matter how hurt they have been in their pasts.

We can therefore say that a contradiction is a viewpoint that allows the bearer of a pattern to perceive the pattern as not present-time reality. It is possible to use contradictions in the workplace in many different ways to help people develop their full potential and contribute effectively to the enterprise.

USING BASIC CONTRADICTIONS IN THE WORKPLACE

In working to build a culture which involves everyone in managing and improving the work of the organization at every level, we need to be cognizant of the major chronic patterns with which women and men battle. The skills we need to develop are aimed at providing a contradiction to those patterns. I have identified five basic skills that are built around this process, which are the following:

O   Focus our attention on other people rather than ourselves.
O   Ask interesting questions and listen with complete respect.
O   Appreciate ourselves and others well and often.
O   Subject everything to critical analysis without personal criticism.
O   Recognize personal criticism and attacks and deal with them elegantly and well.

FOCUS OUR ATTENTION ON OTHER PEOPLE RATHER THAN OURSELVES

Everyone is seeking attention. An early experience of many young people is of never fully being at the centre of their parents' world, yet we all long to feel truly valued. If we examine how the people around us behave in their lives and at work, it becomes clear that probably they have always been doing their best to recover from the adverse effects of never quite having received sufficient attention. Everyone appears to be trying to find someone who will listen to them; whenever two people get together and are not engaged directly in an activity such as work, one or other will begin to talk about what has been or is hard. However, no sooner does one begin to talk than the other, sensing in some way that there is attention around, leaps in and says 'Me too! – I've been hurt like that'. As a consequence neither is listened to or listens well.

Clearly, then, the first skill we need to develop if we are to bring a contradiction to this process is to pay attention to other people rather than to ourselves. In particular, we need to take positive initiatives to listen to people who are different from ourselves, including those who have traditionally not been listened to or encouraged to speak. For example, there is a great deal of evidence that men find it hard to really listen to women talk about their ideas and thinking; so for men to make the effort to encourage women to share their insights and experience is a great contradiction to the effects of the sexism.

However, paying attention to other people is more than just listening well. It is made up of a number of processes, as follows:

○   Decide to attend to other people's issues rather than our own.
○   Communicate to other people that we like them and are interested in them.
○   Put any 'judgementalness' about other people on one side.

DECIDE TO ATTEND TO OTHER PEOPLE'S ISSUES RATHER THAN OUR OWN

Often when we are talking with someone, we notice that they are looking at their watch or looking around the room, and we start to wonder if they really want to be with us. Even the least sensitive person tends to notice this and whenever it happens to me it leaves a feeling of disrespect. Other people only seem able to talk about themselves and to have no interest in anyone else. Apparently, everyone spends a great deal of time focusing on their own difficulties and hence we often find it hard to really connect and be present with other people. And since everyone is so preoccupied with themselves it is understandable that we are constantly looking for opportunities to deal with these past tensions by grabbing every opportunity we get to talk about them.

However, in most situations other people will not be in a position to pay us the attention we need, and continuing to expect it leads to our increasing frustration. So we will be more effective if we decide to only focus attention on our own concerns if someone else has agreed to listen, and in the meantime we should decide to pay attention to other people and their issues.

The best example of excellent leadership of this kind is, in my opinion, that of Nelson Mandela since he was released after spending more than 20 years in prison. To my knowledge, he has not uttered a single complaint about his treatment or voiced a single call for revenge (though many people would have thought he had every reason to) but instead has given his attention to the task in hand.

I worked for many years with the chief executive of a plastics resin company and I often think I learnt more from him about leadership than from any other person I know. He considered that one of the most important parts of his job was developing the senior managers who directly reported to him. He would spend a whole day with each one four times a year and before each meeting he would spend a half day alone, reviewing the managers' progress and planning how to help them improve. Once a month he would meet each operational manager together with his personnel and finance manager to review their business performance. During all of these meetings he gave all of his attention to them. He believed in the importance of their role, he respected each one and he invested the time required to support their development and practice.

THE DECISION TO PAY ATTENTION TO OTHER PEOPLE

The first step is a decision about where we focus our attention. We have to decide to pay attention to the other person rather than to our own concerns and feelings.

This is not always as simple as it sounds. We have to discipline ourselves to be present with them, not to think ahead, getting our response or the next question ready, but to stay in the moment with what they are actually communicating.

Using this skill does not mean we have to pretend that we do not need attention ourselves to deal with our own concerns and struggles. It is an important part of our own ongoing leadership development that we set up situations where another person can pay us attention. Such meetings can usefully take the form of a leadership development meeting (as described in Chapter 13), where at least one other person will pay us attention while we think about what we have done well, what we are struggling with, and how to improve the situation. In my consulting career, I have provided this role for many senior executives who have been unable to find anyone inside their own organization who they feel is appropriate to do this for them.

This process works very well on a reciprocal basis where two people agree to take turns, say for 15 minutes each. Such a relationship is more equal and mutually respectful than the sort of relationship where one person always gives attention and the other always receives it. Establishing support groups can be very helpful. People meet regularly and each person has the opportunity to review their work and plan for improvement. I established support groups in one large leadership development project that I undertook, the groups being led by members of the central management development function.

With the exception of sessions where it is agreed that people will receive some attention on their own difficulties, we need to develop our ability to focus all our attention on other people and the task we are jointly undertaking.

There will be times when people's feelings get in the way of the task. At such times, I have found it useful to stop and put our attention on the people and what is going on and then give them a hand to overcome the blocks that are inhibiting effective work – this can have more impact than simply pushing harder on the task.

The effects of gender conditioning generally mean that women and men are faced with different challenges in this area. Women have historically been expected to pay attention to other people's feelings and struggles. This is part of the caring and parenting role which women have been expected to provide for men, children, elderly people, neighbours and so on. The challenge for women is to take control of these situations and decide whether they wish to focus their attention on other people's difficulties, and avoid being swept into the caring role automatically. We all have a choice and do not have to constantly meet other people's expectations if they do not make sense for us. However, if women decide to do so, then it is important to take complete charge of the situation.

On the other hand, men have not been traditionally encouraged to take the caring role but instead to focus solely on the task in hand. Thus men will need to concentrate their energies more on paying attention to other people, their thinking and their concerns, with the goal of building close, dependable relationships with them.

PAYING ATTENTION TO OTHER PEOPLE IN MORE THAN JUST LISTENING WELL!

O   Decide to attend to other people's's issues rather than our own.
O   Communicate that we are interested in them.
O   Put our judgement of them on one side.
O   Ask 'interesting questions' – these are questions that will release their thinking.
O   'Reflect' back to them a summary of what they say whenever we can to show we have heard.

COMMUNICATE TO OTHER PEOPLE THAT WE LIKE THEM AND ARE INTERESTED IN THEM

One of the consequences of being hurt while growing up and in our adult lives, is that everyone wonders whether they are really liked and approved of. Most people find it hard to believe that other people want to know their opinions. To contradict this feeling we must show people verbally and non-verbally that we like and value them, are interested in being with them and in listening to them.

It is not helpful to be intense or serious about this because this approach is likely to scare people off. It is important to be light-hearted and to have fun. However, people do value warmth and care and it makes a big difference to people's ability to function well. This is particularly important with people who have traditionally faced a great deal of discrimination. I remember a series of interviews with black people and with women in a large Civil Service department where people spoke repeatedly of feeling invisible and left out.

SHOW PEOPLE THAT WE ARE INTERESTED IN THEM

It is not hard to show people that we like them and are interested in what they have to say. We can ask them their opinions. We can say 'Thank you!' to people for the things that they do. We can tell them what we liked about their work or their approach.

We can even tell them that we like them!

PUT ANY 'JUDGEMENTALNESS' ABOUT OTHER PEOPLE ON ONE SIDE

Placing conditions on people that have to be met before they can be accepted hurts them and is likely to reduce their self-esteem. Most of us grew up with parents and teachers who communicated, 'If only you were like Charlie you would be all right!' or 'When you start to work hard, I'll start to treat you well!'. We have to learn how to give up this kind of 'judgementalness' because it leaves people feeling unaccepted and diminished.

Of course, we must distinguish between exercising judgement and being judgemental. Anyone in leadership will have to exercise judgement about situations and people all of the time in order to make good decisions about what to do next. However, most judgementalness is rooted in prejudice, and as I have already described, prejudice is an integral part of and helps perpetuate the system of oppression in which we live. In the case of women and men, our 'judgementalness' usually involves comparing them with how 'real women' or 'real men' should behave.

The challenge is to work with other people without succumbing to our prejudices, in whatever direction they may lie. This means developing the ability to accept people as they are without putting conditions on the relationship.

This is not the way most people behave. Deciding to act in an unconditional manner in our relationships with one another is very unusual in our society where everyone is trying to handle one another's chronic pattern without much understanding of what is going on. Nevertheless, we must aim to be in complete charge of ourselves, building excellent relationships with other people, setting high standards and having high expectations, without resorting to being judgemental.

DEVELOPING THE ABILITY TO BE 'UNCONDITIONAL'

We must begin by learning to recognize when we are acting on a prejudice. Remember, a prejudice is any feeling or opinion not rooted in fact. When we notice that we are thinking, feeling or saying things about people with whom we work or live that are generalizations or based upon a stereotype, we must check our perspective and if it is inaccurate correct it.

ASK INTERESTING QUESTIONS AND LISTEN WITH COMPLETE RESPECT

Many of us believe that the most effective way of influencing other people's behaviour is to tell them what we think they should be doing. We have been trained to devise a solution to every problem presented to us, even though this means we are taking the problem over.

However, as I have argued throughout the book, a key objective of the new leadership is to release the intelligence, creativity and initiative of people at all levels – talking 'at' other people and telling them what to do will not achieve that. In practice it is more effective to help the other person to think independently and to take complete charge of the situation, rather than doing anything that keeps us in control providing the ideas. This offers a very important contradiction to the tradition of people either not being asked or having their thinking ignored once they have given it. We must learn to look at the situation and think about what questions we can ask that will enable people to contribute their best thinking and action.

Once we have asked a question, we need to listen to the other person think through their answer. We will need to give our complete respect and put all judgementalness about the answer to one side. We must give the other person our undivided attention, communicate that we like and value her or him, and ignore any prejudices that we might bring to the situation.

Asking interesting questions works just as well with groups as with individuals. We can use it with an existing management team, a special task force or a one-off meeting, and the group could comprise two people or ten. The challenge is to think of the interesting question that will release the contribution of everyone around the table.

Interesting questions are likely to be of interest to the other person as well as to ourselves and will lead us in a positive direction towards overcoming the difficulties that we face. For example, when we are considering how to solve a problem we have identified in the organization, perhaps the first interesting question is 'Who should be around the table to talk about this?'

Once the meeting begins the interesting questions are those that go right to the heart of the issue – somewhat like asking 'What is the critical path here?' As a starting point, asking one positive question and then a question inviting critical analysis and plans for improvement usually works well. For example, in its simplest form we might ask: 'What is going well since we met last?' It is unusual to pose a positive question and it can play an important part in creating the kind of climate that supports people in taking the initiative to see to it that everything goes well.

A second basic question in a meeting can be: 'What is hard for you, what are you struggling with?' This allows people to focus their thinking on how to improve the situation or the process under discussion. These two questions provide the foundation for the leadership development meeting which is described in the next chapter.

Asking people questions and listening with complete respect is an excellent way of building close, dependable relationships, but some managers make the mistake of thinking that their questions should focus only on non-work issues such as 'How is the family?' or 'I see United won again on Saturday' and so on. Although these may be good questions and interesting exchanges may result, there is a danger that people feel patronized if managers do not also discuss work issues. For example we might ask similar questions to those we would use in a project review meeting: 'What is going well in this section at the moment?' or 'What do you think needs to be improved most in how we do the work?' This approach contributes to building a culture of continual improvement rather than just to pleasant interpersonal relationships.

When people are working together on a project, questions should concentrate on how to remove key blockages. An analogy is when a large number of logs are being carried down river by the current and they jam. There is one 'key log' in the jam, the removal of which would free the whole mass of logs to continue downstream. Thus, we need to ask the question that will lead people to identify the 'key log' and then to remove it. If we cannot identify the 'trigger' question, a good question can be, 'What do you think is the key question, the answer to which would move us forward?'.

Similarly, it can be useful to think in terms of how to create the pre-conditions for change and the question that leads you to think in those terms can make a major difference to planning and achieving a permanent change in people's attitudes or performance.

Listening with complete respect requires us to put aside all judgementalness while people are speaking. Exercising judgement about people's thinking should be done jointly after everyone who wishes to contribute has done so. This follows in the tradition of the brainstorm in which the generation of ideas has to be separated from their evaluation.

We should not be in a hurry to ask another question as soon as someone has finished speaking. We can reflect back a summary of what has been said in order to communicate that we are really listening and to check that we have heard accurately. If we have 'got it' the speaker will be pleased with our ability to understand and then continue on with the exposition, but if we haven't understood we can be corrected.

Another useful tool is to continue to pay attention but to remain silent when someone stops speaking. We need to stay relaxed through the silence, and then the speaker may continue, this time speaking more deeply about the topic. If nothing happens we can ask the question, 'What are you thinking?' and then become silent again. This is a very powerful process and it nearly always encourages the other person to follow the train of thought.

APPRECIATE OURSELVES AND OTHERS WELL AND OFTEN

In Chapter 11 I described the importance of increasing our self-esteem if we are to be effective in our leadership. Low self-esteem is always rooted in the experience of failure and the put-downs that people receive in their lives and the contradiction is to get them to notice what they have done well and to appreciate them ourselves. It is especially important if people have a pattern of heavy self-criticism.

APPRECIATING OURSELVES

We must learn how to appreciate ourselves if we are to become effective in appreciating others. We all need to engage in self-appreciation and we can practise by being completely delighted with ourselves in words, posture, tone, gesture, facial expression and attitude. We can celebrate the inherent human qualities that we have and revel in our achievements. We can decide to accept that we are absolutely fine just as we are – we do not need to prove it or do anything to deserve it. We need to appreciate that each of us has unique gifts to contribute and we need to notice them and start to value and use them.

UNDERTAKING SELF-APPRECIATION

To undertake effective self-appreciation we can begin to appreciate ourselves out loud and without reservation:

- With appreciative, positive words;
- With a proud posture;
- With a pleased expression;
- With a pleased tone of voice.

Undertaking self-appreciation is hard to do and even harder to keep doing. It will feel false or like boasting, or we may fear that it will invite further put-downs. We may feel a pull to justify any positive comments or to introduce certain qualifications and reservations, such as 'Sometimes I can be fairly cooperative if other people give me a chance', instead of 'I am a naturally cooperative person'. If we do this effectively, it will probably bring up feelings about all the times in the past when we did not appreciate ourselves.

APPRECIATING OTHERS

Everyone needs to be appreciated. Some people might say, 'I'm here to do a job, not to be liked!', but being told what people appreciate about me has always helped me to do a better job, and so this process is an integral part of developing a culture of continual improvement. It is a vital part of encouraging other people to contribute their best thinking and efforts. Appreciation is one of the most useful and helpful things we can do in our relationships with others.

People may not seem to like being appreciated – feelings of embarrassment and sometimes sadness may be released causing them to react by laughing, blushing or having even stronger emotions. And, occasionally people are suspicious or mistrustful of our motives. If they react in this way, it is not because we are making them feel like this, but because we are providing a contradiction to times when they have been ridiculed or not taken seriously.

We need to be careful not to be manipulative. The goal is not to persuade people to behave in a particular way but to enable them to emerge from the patterns of self-criticism that most of us have adopted. To do it well we need to develop our insights and skills. We need to pay enough attention to notice what they have done well and appreciate them in specific terms and not just with vague references such as 'You are great!' or 'Well done!' A good example might sound like, 'When you were putting the new program on the computer last week I especially liked the way you met with everybody to plan how we would use it'. We can be enthusiastic about people and their progress.

Moreover, we need to appreciate people particularly in the place that they struggle the most. This does not mean fudging it with false or faint praise; it means paying enough attention (working to understand more of the whole situation) to notice what they did well even when they are making little or no progress or making mistakes. We may notice and appreciate that they have persisted, tried various different approaches or not been hard on other people about it.

THE INTERACTION OF APPRECIATIONS

One of the most positive aspects of appreciating ourselves and appreciating others is that each action feeds and supports the other. If we feel good about ourselves we are better able to feel good towards other people. As people appreciate us, it makes it easier to appreciate ourselves. As people who live and work together increase the amount of appreciation between them, relationships improve and the culture changes.

BECOMING 'SOFT AND FLUFFY'

The most common fear that people express about appreciation is that it will lead to a 'soft and fluffy' climate; people worry that if we are not hard on people they will not improve. However, the main obstacle to people engaging in effective critical analysis is low self-esteem and unless people have sufficient confidence in themselves they are likely to become defensive rather than open to personal review. We need to be pleased with ourselves in order to work on the areas where we need to improve.

SUBJECT EVERYTHING TO CRITICAL ANALYSIS WITHOUT PERSONAL CRITICISM

Applying critical analysis to everything we do is essential if we are to ensure the best possible performance from the people who work in our organizations. We must examine every activity and process and look critically at how they work at present and how they can be improved. The key point is to distinguish between examining people's effectiveness and how much we value them as human beings. We must communicate to people that we like them and appreciate their contribution while rigorously helping them to improve how they carry out their work.

Critical analysis works best when a close, dependable relationship has already been established with another person. If we have appreciated them often for their work and treat them with complete respect at all times, they are more likely to see critical analysis as not being a criticism of them because they already know we like and value them whatever they do.

It is also helpful to have given up the habit of criticizing, blaming or attacking other people when things do not go quite right. If critical analysis does show that someone has made a mistake, we may need to deal with any bad feelings aroused by this, but there is no need to attack or blame the other person. Similarly, if we have made an error, we can apologize, learn from this, and get on with the job of thinking out a better solution.

This is particularly important in our relationships with people who are typically discriminated against. For example, it is extraordinary how often women are seen as the problem when something goes wrong, when, in fact, the problem is rooted in how the system as a whole works.

RECOGNIZE PERSONAL CRITICISM AND ATTACKS AND DEAL WITH THEM ELEGANTLY AND WELL

Many organizations have understood the importance of building a 'no blame' culture as part of their commitment to eliminating discrimination and building continual improvement. However, it is a difficult thing to achieve, and in the meantime we all need to be able to recognize personal criticism and attacks when they come our way and how to deal with them effectively.

RECOGNIZING PERSONAL CRITICISM AND ATTACKS

The first step is to be able to recognize personal criticism and attacks for what they are and discern the difference between them and the process of 'critical analysis'. I define personal criticism as any comment about a person's performance which has the underlying motive of undermining their inherent sense of well-being, and an attack is a more vicious continuation of the same process. It occurs when a person attempts to undermine someone in the eyes of other people. This can be by talking about them behind their back or even by 'organizing' other people against them.

For example, I once worked with two companies, one supplying a product to the other. Senior managers in the customer company would say, 'My supplier never delivers on time. They are a bunch of idiots. They couldn't manage anything.' This was nothing more than organizational slander. It transformed a comment on the performance of the supplier which might or might not be accurate ('*never* delivers on time'), into a number of unhelpful and prejudiced statements with no justification or validity.

In another situation, when I was working as a consultant for a car manufacturer, the training manager told my then boss that he considered a colleague of mine to be unsuitable as a consultant because he was Jewish, and that I was unsuitable because I had dirt under my finger-nails. This feedback was not intended to help us improve (how can you improve from being Jewish?), but to hurt and undermine us! I imagine he was motivated by a fear that we would not look credible to other people in the company and that this would rebound on him, but it was still an attack on us.

There are many factors to take into account when considering how to handle personal criticism and attacks. To begin with we have to be sure that we *are* being undermined. Despite the old joke, 'Just because you are paranoid, doesn't mean that people aren't against you!', our own feelings of not being good enough can sometimes lead us to believe that we are being attacked when we are not. We must be on our guard not to invent negative motives on the part of the other person. Sometimes there is an accurate content to what is being said and we do need feedback in order to do something about it, but the manner of its delivery is blaming or attacking.

Often we are being attacked *because* we have taken the initiative. Hierarchies tend to be quite rigid institutions and people do not like it if other people 'step out of line', even if the behaviour is in the best interest of the organization as a whole. Hence building close, dependable relationships is such an important basis for all action.

However, I believe that, overall, we underestimate how often we are being criticized and attacked. We need to learn to make good judgements about all of these situations and other people's motives, rather than relying on our feelings about what they are doing.

HANDLING ATTACKS ELEGANTLY AND WELL

Once we are able to recognize that we are being attacked, we need to handle the situation effectively, especially if we are to maintain our credibility with other people.

The key points we need to remember are:

O   Stay relaxed and quietly confident.
O   Pay full attention to the other person.
O   Ask interesting questions and listen with complete respect.
O   Develop an appropriate viewpoint.
O   Admit it if we have made a mistake.
O   Encourage the other person to tell us in great detail what we have done wrong.
O   Tell the person to stop it.
O   Organize allies to support us.

Stay relaxed and quietly confident

If we are to handle someone who is criticizing or attacking us effectively, we need to be relaxed and quietly confident in how much we value ourselves and our leadership. For example, we will probably need to listen to the other person for some time while making sure that we do not get defensive at the same time.

Pay full attention, ask interesting questions, and listen with complete respect

The basic approach to handling attacks elegantly and well is to use the skill of listening. Our job is to ask interesting questions and pay sufficient attention to the other person to see if there is anything we need to change, and also what we need to do to help the person concerned move out of a critical frame of mind.

Develop an appropriate viewpoint

It is possible to view most personal attacks as requests for help which are being communicated in code. I have often found it helpful to remember that people are either getting on with the job or indicating what their difficulty is. In a sense, these are the only two possible behaviours. People are either seeing to it that everything goes well, in which case our job is to appreciate them and help them do it even more effectively, or they are indicating what their difficulty is. This might take the form of complaining about and blaming others, and then our job is to work to understand where they are stuck and, if we decide to do so, give them a hand.

It is important here to adopt an attitude of 'not taking it personally'. Basically, we can tell ourselves that we are only ever attacked by a chronic pattern and not by a human being, and if we can decide not to become caught in treating it as a personal matter but something to handle well, we will make great progress.

Admit it if we have made a mistake

Where it is clear we have made a mistake we should admit to it and apologize. For many people, this is a sign of weakness, but I regard it as a sign of great strength. People are always going to make mistakes; indeed, this is how people learn and improve. In a 'no-blame' culture we will regard a mistake as an opportunity to practise critical analysis rather than a reason for an inquisition.

Encourage the other person to tell us in great detail what we have done wrong

In some circumstances it is useful to adopt a practice sometimes called 'negative assertion'. When a person is 'caught' in attacking without reason but the relationship is generally sound, we can ask what it is we have done, tell the person she or he is completely right, apologize and then ask what else we have done wrong, and so on. This has the effect of encouraging the other person to air the bad feelings, but our relaxed apology and invitation to say more defuses the situation. I have witnessed many people gradually dry up when faced with such effective behaviour.

Tell the person to stop it

Occasionally, we are faced with completely irrational attacks which are personal and vindictive and for these a different approach is needed. In these circumstances we need to be clear that the other person has decided to attack us regardless of what is right or wrong, and we can then communicate that we require the attacks to stop immediately and refuse to engage in any further conversation, correspondence or explanation until this happens.

This is not a rejection of the person at a human level but a rejection of the behaviour. On occasions it is not possible to have a rational conversation with another person because she or he is so 'caught' in an attacking pattern, and in these circumstances the appropriate contradiction is to withdraw until the person has decided to stop.

Organize allies to support us

Some attacks are so destructively motivated that anything we do or say will be used against us. Under these circumstances it can be helpful to think with our allies about how they can step in to stop such attacks. This will require them to act with great confidence and skill, using all of the techniques I have described above, on our behalf.

The five basic skills are shown in summarized form below.

THE FIVE BASIC SKILLS OF USING CONTRADICTIONS

○   Focus our attention on other people rather than ourselves: Paying attention is more than just listening. It is about giving our full attention to another person or the job we are doing rather than paying attention to our own concerns.

●   Ask interesting questions and listen with complete respect: Ask people questions which will release their intelligence and then listen with complete respect, rather than coming up with solutions.

○   Appreciate ourselves and others well and often: Encourage contribution and creativity by appreciating ourselves and other people for what they are doing well, particularly in the place that we or they struggle the most.

●   Subject everything to critical analysis without personal criticism: Examine every activity to see how we can improve our performance without engaging in personal criticism of ourselves or others.

○   Recognize personal criticism and attacks and deal with them elegantly and well: Do not assume that we have failed or that it is justified when we are attacked. Sometimes people need help and don't know how to ask, but blame us for not giving them a hand. Sometimes an assertive response is needed to stop the attack.

13

TOOLS AND FORMATS

In the process of building an inclusive organization, I have experimented with many different tools and formats for developing leaders at every level of the organization. These have all been devised to integrate with the new system of leadership proposed in Chapter 10 and the attributes and skills described in Chapters 11 and 12.

Beginning with the tools, we can break them down into two groups:

○   Tools for coaching people;
○   Tools for counselling people.

It may be useful initially to distinguish between those situations where 'coaching' would be helpful and those where a 'counselling' approach is more appropriate. Although most difficulties can be helped by elements of both, coaching is primarily aimed at helping people to take charge of 'task issues' such as technical, informational, methodical or knowledge matters, while counselling concerns 'personal issues' which involve a person's attitudes, feelings, relationships and viewpoints.

There is no clear dividing line between the two processes – they are on a seamless continuum beginning with a focus on the work itself and ending with a focus on the individual undertaking it.

Throughout this chapter, the person receiving help is referred to as the 'client'.

HOW TO RUN A COACHING SESSION

There are a number of basic steps that lead to a successful coaching session. First, agree a 'contract' for the meeting – state the aim of the meeting, make an outline plan, and agree its length. Both people need to work together on the contract so that they can both ensure the meeting goes to plan.

Second, the coach listens to the client's view of the difficulty and then gives her or his view. It is not helpful for the coaching to take the form of a 'conversation', but rather for each person to have their full say, with the client speaking first. Some questions that seem to help are: 'What have you been doing well?' and 'Where do you need to improve?' From the generalized description of where the client needs to improve, draw up a clear statement of the most important issue or issues needing to be tackled.

Third, on the basis of this statement, then move on to 'joint problem solving'. The 'Deming Cycle' 'Plan–Do–Study–Act' is a helpful basis for work throughout these phases.[1] In the cycle, the client and coach can begin by assessing the current situation and then planning what the client will do, setting clear goals and specific actions and devising a checking mechanism so that the client will know if it works (plan). The client can then implement the plan (do), evaluate whether it works and what can be learnt from it (study), and finally decide whether to put any learning into practice in her or his work or to re-cycle (act). Both people can contribute – two heads are often better than one! At this stage, the first steps are obviously to develop a 'plan for improvement', agree the basis for monitoring progress and decide what further support may be helpful.

Fourth, review the meeting. What did the coach do well, what helped, what could have been better? What did the client do well in using the coach's help? Both people speak to these questions – the coach can demonstrate an openness to being coached on her or his coaching in order to improve coaching skills.

If either person becomes stuck at any point or it transpires that the issue is more personal than task, it is always possible to switch to a counselling approach and then return to the coaching role having dealt with whatever feelings are getting in the way, if this is appropriate.

HOW TO RUN A COUNSELLING SESSION

Counselling aims to enable people to express feelings and emotional tensions in order to free up their intelligence, creativity, zest, cooperation, and confidence so that they can deal successfully with challenges in their life and work. The counsellor has the job of enabling the client to function well as an independent, powerful person in the workplace. Therefore, counsellors will need to guard against offering advice because counselling is not primarily concerned with finding solutions to difficulties. After an effective counselling session the client will be better able to resolve the issues being grappled with, decide what to do next, and implement whatever decision has been made.

A thorough understanding of the inherent nature of human beings (outlined in Chapter 4) and the notion of 'contradiction' is very helpful in counselling because one of the significant parts of the counsellor's job is to think about the other person well, be able to distinguish between the person and the patterns being carried, and offer a viewpoint that will contradict where the person is stuck. It is important to differentiate between the ability of a person to think well and take complete and effective charge of their situation, on the one hand, and the way they feel about themselves and the situation that they are in, on the other.

Before beginning, counsellors will find it helpful to remind themselves that their job is to give their complete attention to the client. This means giving up any preoccupation with their own concerns, including any feelings of inadequacy, timidity, fear, or embarrassment about how well they are performing as a counsellor. These kinds of feelings are likely to be evident for most of us but we must not pay any attention to them.

Counsellors need to transmit an attitude to the other person of unconditional approval, encouragement, delight and respect. They will have confidence that the person they are paying attention to is absolutely fine in every way and is capable of overcoming any difficulties.

A typical counselling meeting will probably begin with the same kind of contracting phase as described above for the coaching process. Having established the parameters of the session, the rest of the session will probably go through the following five stages.

First, the counsellor needs to look, listen, observe and think about the client, until it is possible to distinguish clearly between the person and the difficulties that the client may be struggling with. It is most important to see these two aspects clearly and differentiate between them.

Second, very probably these difficulties are rooted in the 'chronic coping patterns' that the client has adopted over time and the counsellor should ask two important questions:

O   What feelings does the client have about her- or himself, other people in the situation or the situation itself?
O   What patterns or rigidities has the client adopted over time in order to be able to 'cope' with such situations?

Third, the counsellor then needs to think of as many ways of 'contradicting' the chronic pattern as possible. This might mean describing the client's situation from an outside perspective, providing an alternative positive viewpoint, coming up with an antidote to the bad feelings, offering the truth about the inherent humanness of the person, or inviting the client to make a decision which would confound the pull of the distress. From such a range of possibilities, the counsellor should select one and try it.

Fourth, make the contradiction. If the conditions are favourable and the contradiction is accurate, the client may well discharge and as a consequence begin to 'see' where her or his thinking has been limited. The client will then be able to use this information to come up with a fresh, new and appropriate response to the situation. In the workplace most people are unlikely to feel safe enough for powerful emotions to be discharged. However, an indication that this process is happening would be the client being able to talk deeply and honestly about the feelings which are being struggled with.

If it is safe enough and a good relationship has built up between the counsellor and the client, deeper feelings may surface. These might include:

O   Laughing – discharging feelings of embarrassment and light fears.
O   Crying – discharging feelings of loss, sadness or grief.

O   Trembling – discharging feelings of fear and terror.
O   Sweating – discharging feelings of fear.
O   Raging – discharging feelings of righteous indignation and anger.
O   Yawning – discharging physical hurts and tensions.

Fifth, the counsellor can then repeat stages one to four, to encourage more discharge. If a contradiction seems to be useful to the client, then it is best to persist with it, but if not, try another one.

Once a person has had the opportunity to talk about her or his difficulties, the person will automatically re-evaluate past painful experiences and begin the process of becoming free from rigid behaviour or irrational attitudes.

This kind of counselling can make a huge difference to the ability of people to take themselves seriously, increase their self-esteem, and to contribute to the very best of their ability. With careful training and systematic preparation for the sessions, all managers should be able to counsel people effectively and well at this depth.

In one project to develop equality of opportunity with which I was involved, we trained 12 harassment counsellors in this approach. They were ordinary people from different levels of the organization and their remit was to help their clients handle their feelings about their situation and then to take charge of it. The counsellors were briefed not to intervene themselves, however difficult the situation seemed to be for their clients. In a subsequent evaluation, they were shown to be very effective and much appreciated by people who had used their services.

Both coaching and counselling figure significantly in the leadership development meeting which is one of the most useful formats developed so far to help managers improve the leadership of their people.

THE LEADERSHIP DEVELOPMENT MEETING

This is an essential and valuable format for developing leadership on-the-job. It should be an integral part of any process of continual improvement in that it concentrates on improving the performance of people as leaders. I have used it as a standard part of the agenda for a business meeting, in specially convened team building meetings, with bosses and subordinates in appraisal sessions, between manager and social worker in supervision sessions, in lunch-time review discussions, or in project work. It can be undertaken in a pair, a threesome or even a group as large as 20.

It is aimed at meeting the leadership needs of people at all levels of responsibility and of all occupations. Leaders seem to find it very helpful to have an opportunity to appreciate themselves for their work, review the situation in which they find themselves, consider what needs to be done, decide what they will do, get help with thinking about how to overcome obstacles, and ask for the assistance of their colleagues in implementing their decisions.

The leadership development meeting is designed to overcome the traditional difficulty of people saying, 'I will do it if you will!', by putting the emphasis on individual responsibility and initiative, although it works most effectively in the context of a group meeting.

All that is required is someone to agree to lead the meeting and a rigorous structure for it. One person needs to take responsibility for the overall process and to see to it that everything goes well, bearing in mind that, at this point, she or he is functioning as a leader of leaders. This person should also take a turn as a participant, handing over the leadership temporarily to an assistant. The format that I use is simple and practical, and while it may be customized to match special needs, the basic structure is guaranteed to work. It comprises six steps, each one beginning with an interesting question. The steps and questions are as follows:

- ○ Step 1 – 'What have you done well since we last met?'
- ○ Step 2 – 'What is the present situation facing us/you?'
- ○ Step 3 – 'What will you do to improve the situation?'
- ○ Step 4 – 'What might get in your way?'
- ○ Step 5 – 'What support will you need to implement your plans?'
- ○ Step 6 – 'What did you like about the meeting and how could it be further improved?

These questions are based on those described earlier in this chapter for coaching and counselling people.

The leadership development meeting forms a fundamental part of the new system of leadership (as described in Chapter 10), and the attributes and skills (described in Chapters 11 and 12) are essential to ensure that the process is fully effective. Giving our full attention to the other person, asking questions and listening (really listening) with complete respect, encouraging and appreciating, coaching and counselling are all invaluable if the meeting is to go well. Moreover, the leadership development process itself can be used to develop skills and effectiveness for leading such meetings if the leader reviews how she or he has performed.

THE STEPS IN MORE DETAIL

Everybody has a turn at responding to a number of questions, is listened to with respect, and is encouraged and appreciated. When the attention is on one person, everybody else is expected to pay attention to that person and help by not drawing attention to themselves, their own ideas or their own problems.

Step 1 – 'What have you done well since we last met?'

Each person answers the question, in turn, and is encouraged to appreciate themselves. If they are stuck or become negative about themselves, the leader may need to assist, possibly by having the other people appreciate the achievements of the person who is answering the question. It is not necessary to name big achievements – any aspect in which the person feels successful is an important starting point.

Step 2 – 'What is the present situation facing us/you?'

Each person speaks to the question in turn. There is no attempt to debate or reach agreement since different viewpoints are important. Each respondent is encouraged to share their thinking and their assessment of the situation.

I often find it helpful to ask people to focus on two subsidiary questions rather than just on the main question. They are:

O   What are the strengths that we have in the situation at the moment?
O   What are the key difficulties we face?

These questions help people to focus first on the positives and only then on what needs to be improved.

It can be helpful if people prepare for these questions before attending the meeting. Indeed, where people have others reporting to them, it can be very empowering to pose the question of those people and thus be thoroughly briefed oneself.

Step 3 – 'What will you do to improve the situation?'

Each person is invited to consider and then share, in turn, the personal initiatives they will take – not what others should do, or what the team should do but what they will do personally in order to take the initiative. They may plan to convene a team meeting or bring important issues to another person's attention, but the focus is always on their own individual initiative in the situation.

It can be useful to focus this step on getting people to make a decision – in doing this they are essentially deciding to see to it that everything goes well. So, for example, they might say 'I decide to see to it that …' and then consider the consequences of this decision in terms of specific actions. Some of the proposals for women and men to develop their leadership outlined in Chapters 7 and 9 may provide a useful starting point for this phase.

Another useful tool is to encourage people to think about their vision of how they would like things to be, and then to use the planning process described in Chapter 10 in order to achieve their vision.

Step 4 – 'What might get in your way?'

The emphasis here should mainly be on the internal blocks and struggles each person faces in carrying out Step 3. If external difficulties arise it is possible to re-cycle back to Step 2 and include them as part of the description of the present situation, refocus on what the person will do to deal with the difficulty, and then return to the internal struggles.

The leader's role is crucial – coaching and counselling each person on where they might struggle by using the processes described above on coaching and counselling. The person leading the session can also take a turn by appointing someone to act as coach and counsellor to her- or himself.

The process works best for each person to take Step 4 immediately after Step 3, rather than passing to the next person and having two separate rounds.

Step 5 – 'What support will you need to implement your plans?'

Here, each person has the opportunity to consider what support they might need from colleagues in order to implement the plans they have made, and to ask and get people's agreement to giving it. However, this should not become a 'dependent' agreement in which people begin to say that something will only be done if someone else provides support.

Step 6 – 'What did you like about the meeting and how could it be further improved?'

A leadership development meeting can be closed by thanking everyone for their contribution and asking each person what they liked about the meeting and how it could be further improved.

After several meetings, people's skills and insights into the process improve and the meetings themselves become more effective and efficient. As the meetings get better they have an increasing impact on the effectiveness of people, teams and organizations. Over time it is possible to introduce these processes into the ongoing life of the organization as a natural occurrence.

THINKING ABOUT HOW TO USE CONTRADICTION ON A DAILY BASIS IN THE WORKPLACE

Once we understand the process of contradiction, we can begin to use it on a daily basis to build the kind of culture that will bring out the best in people. I think we can say with some certainty that people will be able to give of their best when the following conditions apply:

O   There is a climate of relaxed approval and people are appreciated for trying, and specifically for what they do well when they try.

O   People are helped to set appropriate goals for improvement for themselves.

O   People are encouraged to be pleased with their successes.

O   People are able to make mistakes without incurring recrimination.

O   People are thoroughly listened to about what they find hard and are not criticized for it.

O   People are helped to identity the key difficulties that make things hard for them.

O   People are coached and counselled effectively to assist them eliminate their difficulties.

When these conditions are patiently and carefully built and nurtured they provide a fundamental contradiction to the difficulties that people typically bring to their work. They allow people to begin to flourish and slowly but surely, the real potential of people will begin to show.

REFERENCES

1.   *Out of the Crisis*, E.W. Deming (Cambridge, MA: MIT Centre for Advanced Engineering Study, 1986).

14

A PROGRAMME FOR CHANGE

Building an inclusive organization requires a huge change in values and behaviour at every level of our organizations. It will not be achieved overnight – introducing such changes in practice and culture can take up to five years in a small enterprise and often closer to ten in medium to large organizations. This transformation can best be achieved by developing a planned, organization-wide programme aimed at *creating a new leadership initiative*.

If the aim of this programme is to build an organization that reaches systematically to include everyone who works in it, it will need to empower people right at the 'bottom' of the organization to take charge of their work and improve how it is done. Moreover, it will be necessary to take positive action to ensure that the people who are most often excluded are included and encouraged to contribute. In order to prepare the organization as a whole to undertake this change, the programme should be directed first at the top team and then extended to senior and middle managers before involving everyone in the organization. People in the personnel and training functions will need special attention because of their particular roles in leading the organization.

The programme needs to be designed to increase people's knowledge and understanding of the theoretical underpinning to the change, help them to review and, where appropriate, change their attitudes and develop their skills. It is about effecting a permanent change in people's attitudes, competence, and the way in which things get done in every part of the organization. It is aimed at developing the ability of people at every level to see the whole situation and to make the decision to see to it that absolutely everything in it goes well, and then to see that this practice becomes *the way* of doing things.

Such an approach fits very effectively alongside strategies to improve the quality of products and processes through continual improvement. Historically, these have often focused on involving people in looking systematically at how to improve their performance, but there is rarely a focus on the ways in which some people are excluded from contributing. However, the only difference between quality and equality is the letter 'e' and if we want people to become more customer focused we need to ensure that we treat them well in their role as employees first.

There are six areas that will need attention in organizations planning such an approach. They are the following:

O   Developing top management commitment and vision.
O   Reviewing personnel policies and practice.
O   Training the trainers.
O   Leadership development with managers throughout the organization.
O   Team building with work teams at all levels.
O   Involving everyone in the new leadership initiative.

DEVELOPING TOP MANAGEMENT COMMITMENT AND VISION

For such a programme to be successful in the longer term, it requires the understanding and commitment of top management. The primary role of top management in any organization is to establish the environment in which work takes place. They are unable to dictate everything that happens, however many controls they put into place, but they are able to be a model of the values and behaviour that they want other people to adopt.

In order to do this they will need to review their own approach, adopt the new philosophy and be ready to initiate a fundamental change in their approach to leadership. They are likely to find that most aspects of leadership they have believed in and valued up until this point will be challenged and will have to undergo a massive transformation. I have found that it frequently takes a person such as a chief executive or a senior manager two or three years of hard work to really begin to understand for themselves the change I am proposing, and to become congruent with it in their own behaviour.

Members of top management will also need to appreciate how long it takes to initiate a culture change in an organization. As I said above, the sheer inertia and resistance to change of the modern enterprise means that a fundamental change in organizational culture and practice is unlikely in less than five to ten years. Top management will need to remain constant in pursuit of their goals in the face of many difficulties and set-backs.

They must understand that introducing these changes requires a great investment of people's time and this will incur a cost that needs to be understood and agreed. Moreover, beginning with top management themselves, people at all levels will need time to review how they operate and then training to help them be more effective. New processes of appraisal and supervision will need to be installed. Personnel practices must be overhauled and brought into line with the goal of building an inclusive organization. All of these activities will incur costs and top management needs to be aware of them and to make the long-term commitment to invest.

The role of top management in this process is similar to its role in any other organizational transformation activity and work will need to begin on a number of specific tasks, which are the following:

○   Develop a vision of what an inclusive organization would mean in the current context.
○   Develop a 'charter for employees'.
○   Develop a clear and achievable equal opportunities policy.
○   Develop a 'customer charter' about service delivery to customers.
○   Develop an organization-wide strategy for introducing these changes.

DEVELOP A VISION OF THE FUTURE

Chapter 11 described how to develop a shared vision of the future. Top management can adopt this approach, beginning with each person working first on answering the question: 'How would I like things to be if they were meeting my deepest held values and beliefs?' and then building a shared vision from this individual thinking.

In the context of an inclusive organization, I have sometimes asked this question in the form of:

*How would I like this organization to look in, say, five years' time
if it were meeting my deepest held values and beliefs about
including everyone who works in it in every aspect of its functioning?*

The vision statement produced from this work is first written up and then improved by one or two members of the group over the next two or three weeks, bringing it back to the team for review and further improvement until everyone is able to sign up to it.

I helped the chief executive and top team of a defence sector company to develop a statement of their ideal future. This was part of a two-and-a-half day workshop which had begun on the first evening with the presentation of feedback about the present situation which had been collected from interviews with team members undertaken in the three weeks before the event.

Members of the group were invited to think overnight about their personal vision for the company in five years' time and then in the morning they were given time to prepare a detailed statement which had to be broken down into short sentences. Each sentence was to be written on a small 'post-it' and then all of the 'post-its' were placed upon a wall.

The team members were then invited to begin grouping these sentences into similar 'areas of interest', continuing until there was a high level of collective agreement about the groupings. Each area of interest was then given a title which represented the common interest expressed in it, and team members then devised a sentence or two that fully summarized each area. Next, the titles were presented to the team as a whole and we checked to see if everybody felt represented and then moved to asking for and obtaining team agreement. This was then adopted as the top team vision statement.

It will also be necessary to develop or revisit the organization's mission or statement of aim to ensure that it embraces the notion of 'inclusion' fully and elaborating it if it does not.

DEVELOP A 'CHARTER FOR EMPLOYEES'

Work will need to be undertaken to develop a policy on staff care that can be turned into a 'top management charter for employees'. In most situations this activity can be initiated in the personnel function, but it must be adopted and backed by top management if it is going to make any impact.

The charter should define how employees can expect to be treated as members of the organization by people in management and colleagues. Such a statement makes the requirements on everyone explicit from the outset, and acts as a reassurance to people who may suffer mistreatment that the organization will support them by dealing with it.

If the charter is to make a difference in ensuring that everybody is included it needs to pay particular attention to the issue of harassment, particularly of members of groups that have typically been vulnerable to harassment. Harassment is one of the most general forms of discrimination in the workplace and a major obstacle to building an inclusive organization. It represents unacceptable behaviour wherever it occurs and ranges from verbal to physical to sexual in nature. At work, the harassment of members of any group by colleagues, bosses or subordinates creates a negative and hostile culture which excludes people and is particularly hurtful to those who are the target of such behaviour.

Harassment creates an environment that can limit employees' ability to give of their best, alienate the person being harassed and consequently increase staff turnover. When not dealt with, such behaviour can result in the victim resigning her or his job and the organization becoming known as a hostile place for members of that particular group to work.

Historically, people have often felt unable to complain about harassment, or if they have complained they have been ignored, or even worse, there has been a general acceptance that such behaviour has to be 'tolerated'. Now, many organizations incorporate a 'code of practice on harassment' with a well-defined grievance procedure as a central plank in their staff care policy. This code is aimed at dealing with the different forms of harassment and ultimately eradicating them from the workplace.

Sexual harassment creates a negative atmosphere in the workplace, and will reduce working effectiveness, particularly for women who tend to be the main victims, but actually for all employees. At the present time, sexual harassment is generally defined as any behaviour that is regarded as unwanted by the person on the receiving end and has a sexual overtone. It is vital for top management to make explicit its opposition to sexual harassment by ensuring that any complaint is dealt with satisfactorily, and that proper support is given to the complainant.

Once the staff care charter has been developed, a clear written statement needs to be made available to everyone who works in the enterprise. People's reactions are unlikely to be very positive at first. Whenever such documents are developed, the hopes and expectations of ordinary people in the enterprise are raised even though the cynics among them doubt that top management is really genuine. Every action taken by management after that point is then analysed and found wanting and the commitment of top management to implement the charter is essential if people are to eventually believe it.

DEVELOP A CLEAR AND ACHIEVABLE EQUAL OPPORTUNITIES POLICY

A clear statement of policy on equal opportunities practice which is fully owned by top management is essential. Such statements have become commonplace during the past ten years, and many people consider that they have become meaningless in most situations. However, developing a policy and winning the commitment of everyone in the organization to it is a vital step in the process of building an inclusive organization.

A colleague and I began an organization-wide programme of training on equal opportunities for a government agency with two workshops for the top management team. The first workshop of three days' duration was designed to provide an introduction to the key issues surrounding gender, race and disability. The second workshop lasted two days and was aimed primarily at enabling the team to develop an equal opportunities policy statement.

The initial stages of the policy development workshop were very similar to those described above for developing a vision statement in the defence company. On this occasion, however, once the different ideas had been generated and captured on sheets of flip-chart paper, I took the sheets and analysed the content, identified the key areas, and turned them into statements that embraced all of the ideas generated by the group. These were then presented back to the team, agreed in broad principle and then handed to the Personnel Director for him to turn into a finished version for publication back in the workplace.

DEVELOP A 'CUSTOMER CHARTER' ABOUT SERVICE DELIVERY TO CUSTOMERS

Customer charters are also a wonderful idea that have been somewhat discredited by cynicism about unattainable targets and difficult-to-believe performance statistics. Nevertheless, every organization needs to communicate its commitment to providing excellent service to its customers and to detail the standards by which that service can be judged.

In the context of an inclusive organization, this is particularly important. Many organizations still regard the special needs of 'minority customers' as a nuisance and do not take the opportunity to involve and delight those people with the products or services they can provide. Take, for example, the issue of safety for women in car parks late at night. Any organization that recognized the particular concerns of such customers, found ways of asking for their help in identifying the key problem areas, and then developed, published and implemented a policy of making car parks safe would be greatly admired and appreciated by *everyone* because making the place safer for one group improves it for all.

It is the responsibility of top management to lead in this by asking for and backing work on a customer charter that identifies the most important desires of customers and promises to deliver them.

I recall working with the Director of a large software team developing a command and control system for a government department. We invited the customer project manager to attend the first evening of a performance improvement workshop in order to give the project team feedback about their performance. I met with him beforehand to help him prepare and then encouraged him to talk firmly about what they had done well and later about what could be improved.

The following morning I read back notes I had made of the key points to the group and then we began work to understand, explore the implications of the feedback, and then to develop a charter for future behaviour towards the customer.

We devised a working version at the workshop before moving on to developing a strategy for improvement, but when the charter had been polished to perfection and agreed by the group as a whole, the Director invited his customer to a further meeting to be briefed on the charter. The customer then took this statement back to his own group to brief them and to consider how they could respond effectively to the initiative.

DEVELOP AN ORGANIZATION-WIDE STRATEGY FOR INTRODUCING THESE CHANGES

Finally top management need to develop and agree an organization-wide strategy for introducing these changes, which must include how to communicate their thinking and decisions down through the organization in ways which are convergent with the values that underpin the programme as a whole.

This strategy will need to include changes in the role and behaviour of the personnel and training function, how to use temporary groupings such as training sessions and teambuilding workshops to enable managers at senior, middle and junior levels to embrace the change, and how to involve people at all levels of the organization in the process.

REVIEWING PERSONNEL POLICIES AND PRACTICE

The policies and practices developed in the personnel function are some of the most important determinants of whether people are included or excluded in the organization. The structures of people management are developed in personnel through recruitment, promotion, performance appraisal, payment systems and so on. Personnel in an organization based upon traditional leadership has often fulfilled the function of a police force, setting the parameters of acceptable organizational behaviour and rewarding or punishing people depending on whether or not they *comply* with its requirements.

For example, I recall working in a major US-owned international telecommunications company, where the personnel function fed top management in the United States up-to-date information about what was happening in the United Kingdom business. In particular, they secretly supplied regular updates on individual managerial performance and these reports decided people's future career.

Because of the negative image created by this history, personnel in the inclusive organization has to undergo a paradigm shift as great as that confronting top management. It will need to begin valuing and cherishing the contribution that employees at all levels can make to the business. A review of whether and how people are included and excluded is essential and needs to examine whether or not discrimination and prejudices have, consciously or subconsciously, become institutionalized into the organization's policies. Personnel is in a position to provide a significant lead to other managers towards the new leadership.

Once it has begun this shift, personnel can help the top management team with preparatory work on many areas including the staff care policy and the equal opportunities policy. It can then monitor and assess how effectively these are being introduced and practised.

The personnel function of a government headquarters function asked colleagues of mine to undertake a survey of its performance in delivering its equal opportunities policy. It set up a steering group of representatives from several of the groups named in the policy statement and this steering group defined the brief, chose the consultants and managed their work.

The survey comprised interviews with a wide cross-section of people in the department and the results of these interviews were then turned into a report with recommendations on next steps. This report was presented to the steering group which, with our help, then planned how to present the findings to top management.

TRAINING THE TRAINERS

It is increasingly understood that training makes a major contribution to any programme of planned change. However, trainers, just like anyone else in a common enterprise, are likely to have been brought up in the culture of traditional leadership. Therefore, people in the training function need to be trained in the basic concepts and practice of the new leadership initiative and in an understanding of the role of oppression as a block to organizational effectiveness and leadership, and then to begin intensive trainer development to enable them to transform how they deliver training themselves.

Despite my preference for beginning with top management, often this has not been possible. While this situation is never ideal, I have begun the whole programme with work based in the training function, and then worked with the top management team at a later stage. With good leadership in the training function this can work quite well.

The management development function serving a number of government departments invited myself and a colleague to begin a programme of training on leadership and gender awareness. On our recommendation, they arranged the training to include equal numbers of women and men, and about two-thirds of each group at the first three workshops were from the various training functions located in each department.

On completion of the basic training, the participants were invited to join ongoing support groups facilitated by members of the central management development team. Later the trainers in the groups were invited to attend two further advanced leadership development workshops which included intensive coaching on the leadership of training events and exploration of other areas of discrimination and prejudice.

LEADERSHIP DEVELOPMENT WITH MANAGERS THROUGHOUT THE ORGANIZATION

Once the top management team has developed its own vision of the future, its staff care policy, its equal opportunities policy, and its strategy plan for implementation, it will need to communicate this to all levels of the enterprise as an integral part of the annual planning process. It can then begin the process of cascading these new ideas and practices down through the organization.

LEADERSHIP DEVELOPMENT FOR MIDDLE MANAGERS

People in middle management positions are often the strongest supporters of the traditional approach to leadership and therefore the most resistant to a new leadership initiative. They sometimes feel they have the most to lose from any change, because their personal power has been based historically on their ability to dominate and coerce people on behalf of top management. Moreover, in recent years middle managers have become the target for major restructuring with whole swathes being eliminated. This kind of behaviour on the part of top management obviously leads middle managers to feel vulnerable and threatened, and they will need special support to review their own role and to develop a new practice for themselves.

Therefore, it is vital to introduce the concept of an inclusive organization to these key managers, help them to understand what it will mean for them and then invite them to work towards the vision of an organization in which everyone is fully included. To help them, I have found it essential to brief them carefully and then offer them the opportunity to participate in a leadership development programme.

My approach to achieving this in one computer software company was to plan and deliver a series of workshops aimed at preparing middle managers to practise the new system of leadership in their own workplace. We had at least one senior manager present at each workshop as a representative of the top team and participants comprised a diagonal slice of people from different functions and levels.

The training included the following elements:

O   Presentations on the concept of an inclusive organization.
O   Presentations on the new system of leadership.
O   Individual work to develop the middle managers' own vision of the future.
O   Work to develop and improve their ability to deploy the key attributes and skills.
O   Developing plans for their return to work.

Chapter 15 contains more about training for middle managers.

TEAM BUILDING WITH WORK TEAMS AT ALL LEVELS

Whenever two or three participants from a given work team have completed the leadership development training, I recommend a performance improvement and team building workshop for their team in order to maximize the transfer of learning, embed the concepts and skills of the new leadership initiative, and assist them to plan together how they will manage from now on.

In a programme undertaken in an automobile company, we planned team building workshops for each function to follow attendance at the leadership development training. In plant engineering, I spent a half day with the manager reviewing what he had learnt at the workshop and planning how best to work with his team.

We decided upon an initial half-day review meeting with the team as a whole, followed by a two-day workshop. At the first half day we used the leadership development meeting format to review the present situation and identified key areas for improvement. At the workshop we created a shared vision of the future, developed a code of management practice which would be used as the basis for future management behaviour towards their staff and then worked on improving participants' coaching skills.

INVOLVING EVERYONE IN THE NEW LEADERSHIP INITIATIVE

In the final phase of the programme, the initiative must be spread throughout the organization. Each manager will need to lead a process of continual improvement by setting up the leadership development meetings described in Chapter 13 with his or her own team.

When people meet to do this it reduces their isolation and improves relationships. It enables the leader to develop individual competence, coordinate people's individual efforts and reduces the need to spend time checking on whether people have done what they agreed to do. This process can then extend into systematic activity aimed at improving the performance of everyone engaged in the common task of providing high quality products and services to all customers.

This is the heart of the strategy. This is what all of the work up until this point has been aimed at – namely, getting to the point where people at junior levels are able to develop their own leadership and participate in the process of continual improvement. This is where the mass of people, ignored and undervalued, begin to contribute to the future of the common enterprise, its goals and processes.

15

TRAINING FOR WOMEN AND MEN

❖

T raining on issues of gender for women and men has been one of the most important and exciting innovations made towards building an inclusive organization during the past ten years. Work in this area is becoming more widespread as organizations begin to understand and value, first, the importance of women and then, the importance of helping men to understand their role in building an inclusive organization.

Initially, during the early 1980s, the top management of many organizations launched and supported organization-wide programmes aimed at putting women at the centre of the business and these programmes had limited success. Subsequently, it was recognized that it would be necessary to help key gatekeepers – mostly male – review and change their own behaviour.

This led to the development of training for women and men working together, aimed at helping them to understand how gender conditioning influences behaviour in the workplace and to develop an effective leadership. Probably, most of such training has taken place in the public sector, but increasingly private sector organizations are experimenting with training on gender awareness for women and men.

In recent years, I have led several workshops for existing management teams where all or most of the team members have been male and we have adopted a positive action strategy of 'promoting' an appropriate number of senior women colleagues into the event. While such workshops are always extremely difficult, they provide a real-time opportunity for male managers to hear about the experience of the women they work alongside, to share about themselves and to work together to plan change.

Workshops normally comprise around six women and six men and are led by a female and male trainer, although I have been involved in several with 24 participants and four trainers. Workshops for operational managers normally last three days and often have a follow-up. The training of trainers usually involves attendance at a basic five-day workshop followed by two further intensive training workshops of four or five days each after which the trainers may work as assistants in further workshops.

The early workshops were led by people with a history in interpersonal skills training and built upon that approach. The workshops brought members of both sexes together in small groups to 'confront' one another. I have vivid memories of the first workshop of this kind in which I was involved – by the end of the first day the men had become thoroughly defensive and the women were furious with them. It was very unproductive and did not add one jot to their joint understanding; indeed, some people had their negative views about the other group reinforced.

After these early experiences some of us undertook a systematic review of our approach and began to apply the perspectives described in Chapter 5 on how oppression works in organizations. On the basis of these insights, we developed two important principles on which all of our subsequent training has been based. They are as follows:

O   Women and men need to meet first in separate-sex groups in order to build trust and develop their understanding of how internalized oppression divides and sets the members of their own group against one another.

O   Women and men both need the opportunity to speak to one another about their experience of discrimination and prejudice and be able to ask for support from the other group while they are listened to with complete respect.

WOMEN AND MEN NEED TO MEET FIRST IN SEPARATE-SEX GROUPS

As we developed our understanding of oppression and the role of 'internalized oppression, we began to recognize that it was helpful to begin the training with people in single-sex groups of between four and eight people, with a trainer in each group, to explore their common experiences and consider how to communicate to the other group. The reason for this was that women and men tend to have different levels of consciousness about the existence and effects of oppression upon the lives of women. Most women acquire some awareness of sexism as they grow up and in their workplaces, even if they do not call it that, but, it seems that most men either do not notice or actively deny that sexism exists at all. Moreover, very few men have ever conceived that there is an oppression of men and that its purpose is to divide and set men against one another and to prepare them for the oppressor role in sexism.

Putting women and men together before men have had the chance to begin their own exploration often exacerbates this difficulty, as we experienced in the early workshops. The most unaware men are likely to campaign strongly against the ideas and other men may well 'follow' them – and women, understandably, become increasingly hostile.

We therefore proposed limiting the bringing of women and men together to the presentation of keynote theory topics until each group had begun to build trust and understand the way in which internalized oppression operates between its own members. Thus, if in the theory presentations we talked about the inherent nature of human beings and the cycle of oppression, this would then provide the basis for exploration and trust building in the small groups. Once the groups had begun to understand and combat their own internalized oppression, it became possible for them to start listening to the experience of the other group. We found this worked well and overcame the difficulties experienced in earlier workshops.

WOMEN AND MEN NEED TO DISCUSS THEIR EXPERIENCE OF OPPRESSION WITH EACH OTHER

Once a climate of trust has been established within the separate-sex groupings, it is possible to begin the work of increasing trust and understanding between the two groups. This is best done by the members of each group being given the opportunity to speak to the other group about a number of questions such as:

O   Their experience of oppression as they grew up and in their adult lives.
O   How they have internalized the oppression and its effects on their lives.
O   What they will need to do for themselves to move forward.
O   What they will need from the other group to support them in moving forward.

Each group needs to plan beforehand how to behave when the other group is sharing its thinking, and then draw on the skills described in Chapter 12 while the two groups are together. If one group is able to give its undivided attention to the other group while it is speaking and listen to its message with complete respect, the foundations will be built for a new level of trust and mutual understanding. This is particularly important for men, because it is the experience of most women that men find it difficult to listen to them talk about their interests and concerns.

THE WORK WITH WOMEN

Much work has been done to develop positive action training for women during the past 20 years. Women such as Pauline Farrell, when she worked at the Civil Service College, and Rosemary Brennan, working as an independent consultant, have identified the key issues and developed training designs that are consistently successful in encouraging women to challenge their internalized oppression and take full leadership in every situation. A large number of women have now experienced single-sex training and extensive evaluation shows that they uniformly welcome and appreciate the training which makes a huge difference to their effectiveness.

The goals of the training may be summarized as follows:

O   To help women increase their confidence in their own abilities and potential, and to have high expectations of themselves.

○ To help women set goals for themselves in their current work and in their career overall.

○ To give women any knowledge and skills that have been denied to them because of their membership of the oppressed group but which are needed to achieve those goals.

○ To give women the opportunity to 'experience and practice' in the actual situation to which they aspire.

Working with women in the context of training for women and men together is an extension of this women-only training. In general, the possibility of defensiveness, particularly on the part of the men, and the increase in tension that results, can severely impair building a safe and effective learning climate; however, this provides an excellent opportunity for women to take charge and neither revert to subservience nor resort to attack.

Effective work with women in a leadership or gender awareness workshop for women and men must be rooted in the principles outlined in Chapters 6 and 7. To recap these are as follows:

○ Women as a group are oppressed by men acting as the agents of sexism.

○ This oppression comprises a range of institutionalized discriminatory practices and behaviours which are justified by prejudice and negative stereotypes about women.

○ Women resist this oppression, but, to the extent that they are unable to resist, they could be said to internalize it.

○ As part of the stereotyping process, the way a woman is supposed to look and a set of behaviours have been defined as criteria to judge whether a woman is able to make it as a 'real woman', and young women are brought up to compare themselves with these criteria.

○ No women will be able to meet these criteria, but every woman will be expected to try, with praise if they do and punishment if they do not. This process is called 'gender conditioning'.

○ In order to challenge this internalized oppression and gender conditioning women will need to:

    – Challenge all the ways they have ended up feeling badly about themselves by deciding to appreciate themselves just as they are without limit or reservation.

    – Challenge all the ways they have ended up feeling badly towards other women by deciding to treat every other woman with complete respect

    – Challenge all the ways women mistreat themselves by promising to remember they are valuable beyond measure and deciding to never ever mistreat themselves again in any way whatsoever, however badly they may feel.

    – Challenge all the ways they mistreat other women by deciding to never again mistreat any other woman in any way whatsoever, but instead to reach to build the best possible relationship they can based upon mutual respect and support.

- Challenge all the ways that women allow themselves to be mistreated by deciding they will never again agree to be mistreated but will act instead to fully take charge of whatever situation they face.
- Challenge all the ways that women allow other women to be mistreated by deciding to be an ally to every other woman in their efforts to eliminate all mistreatment of themselves by standing up for them and in supporting them to stand up for themselves.
- Challenge the core of women's internalized oppression by deciding to settle for nothing less than absolutely everything.

When these principles are acted on, women are able to have very successful learning experiences in joint sessions with men.

WORKING WITH MEN

During the past 15 years I have worked with several hundred men both in leadership development workshops for women and men and in workshops for men alone, and many of them report a fundamental shift in their understanding and approach. It has led to excellent results in their lives and in their leadership.

It is sensible to be thoughtful about the recruitment of men for this training. While the idea of work with men has gained increasing credence since I began this work, it is still a very new concept and it does not, as yet, have widespread acceptance. Therefore, only those men who are likely to be favourably disposed to the training and who are likely to be ready to take leadership on the issue in their work and lives should be invited.

Moreover, it is essential that men are volunteers into such training and that no one is pressured to attend 'because it would be good for them'. While every man is reachable, given time, having someone present in the workshop who rigidly disagrees with the ideas it is based on or who does not really want to be there can make it difficult for others to learn well.

BASIC ASSUMPTIONS OF THE TRAINING

In developing this new training I had to review and examine all of the assumptions I made as an experienced trainer and consultant concerning how to help people to learn. I had to examine my own beliefs about the inherent nature of men and the conditions needed for them to claim back their inherent nature, as outlined in Chapter 9. Effective work necessitates the rigorous application of these principles whatever the situation.

First, it is necessary to recall the key aspects of the theory outlined in Chapter 8:

O   Men are oppressed, though not by women or children. There is a systematic mistreatment of men in our culture that trains them to act as 'warriors', 'providers' and to become the agents of sexism towards women.

This mistreatment almost always includes violence, abuse and humiliation. In particular, it is aimed at stopping them from feeling how they feel.

O   Underlying this mistreatment is an anti-male conditioning that regards men's lives as dispensable, exploitable and of little intrinsic value other than as workers.

O   Men internalize this mistreatment and conditioning and disconnect themselves from their inherent nature. In the end they accept that the way they were taught to act, both towards themselves and towards other men and women, is the right way to act.

O   As a consequence, men usually end up feeling numb, insensitive to what they and others feel, competitive and aggressive, and rarely able to place their own or others human interests first.

It is therefore crucial to adopt assumptions about men's inherent nature that contradict the effects of men's oppression. I choose the viewpoint that men are inherently and potentially good, intelligent, loving, cooperative and powerful human beings. They are enthusiastic and love life. They are not inherently arrogant, domineering, patronizing, boring or stupid.

Given how different these assumptions are from the general view, training for men will be most successful when a climate is created that reflects their inherent nature. Remind them that they are inherently intelligent, cooperative, loving and powerful. Appreciate them for their achievements, support them in their struggles to get things right, and maintain the highest expectations about their ability to improve their lives still further. It means never abandoning them.

In practice, I only experience difficulties in doing this work when I forget to act on these assumptions from the start or when I forget to assume them when a difficulty occurs.

DESIGNING A WORKSHOP FOR WOMEN AND MEN

Putting all of the ideas explored above into practice has produced a design for the workshops that includes the following:

O   All participants develop their own vision of how they would like working relationships to be between women and men.

O   The presentation of theory to the whole group.

O   Individual work on key issues in the safety of a small, single-sex group led by a trainer.

O   Work in pairs to review and listen to one another.

DEVELOPING A VISION

The first step is for all participants to develop a vision of how they would like their working relationships to be with members of the other sex if they were meeting their deepest held values and beliefs. Thinking positively before starting work on the key issues is an important contradiction to the fears that most people bring to such a training.

THE THEORETICAL PRESENTATIONS

It was apparent early in our work that people either have very little information or are thoroughly misinformed about how leadership is affected by oppression in general and gender conditioning in particular. Therefore, a number of key theoretical presentations on the issues involved are needed.

These sessions best comprise the presentation of theory, followed by people meeting in pairs to review what they have learnt, followed by time for people to share what they heard that was useful and to comment or ask any questions about it. I often give people the space to talk through difficulties or disagreements in the whole group, and I sometimes demonstrate particular aspects of the theory by giving an individual space to talk about her- or himself using the attention of the group as a whole.

A typical workshop might contain the following theory presentations:

O   The importance of building an inclusive organization.
O   The role of leadership in building an inclusive organization.
O   The new system of leadership, the key attributes and the basic skills of effective leadership.
O   The inherent nature of human beings.
O   How discrimination and prejudice work in organizations to undermine effectiveness.
O   The effects of gender conditioning upon women and men's leadership.
O   What it means to reclaim personal power.
O   How to build effective alliances with members of one's own and the other sex.
O   Building a vision of the future and planning how to get there.

Trainers need to be completely familiar with all the information presented and be able to present it enthusiastically and simply. They must be sufficiently skilled to handle disagreements and attacks in a relaxed and easy way.

WORK IN THE SMALL GROUPS

Small group meetings are interspersed between the theory presentations. The groups normally comprise between four and eight female participants with a female trainer, and between four and eight male participants with a male trainer. Sometimes a member of the in-house training team joins as an assistant which in turn can form part of her or his training to become a trainer.

Initially, follow a similar approach in both groups, but, as the work with each group unfolds, the trainer can facilitate work on the particular issues that its members raise.

I find the most successful approach is to think about and ask the group interesting questions and then encourage each person to respond. This facilitates two processes at once – participants are able to share important information about themselves, often for the first time in their lives, and at the same time they can see their experience is common to other women and men. The trainer can also answer the questions, sometimes taking the first turn to speak and other times in the middle or last, according to the needs of the group.

In a typical workshop, the women's trainer might encourage the group members to tell one another about:

O   What they like about being female and how they are proud of themselves as women and as leaders.
O   Their life story as one of triumph over adversity.
O   What their experience has been of being brought up to see themselves primarily as carers.
O   What they were taught about their role in society and in organizations, particularly in relation to leadership.
O   What their experience is of being encouraged to settle for less than everything in their lives.
O   What has been the impact of this conditioning on their relationships with other women and with men, and on their attitude to their own leadership.
O   What they like, appreciate and admire about the other women in the group, including themselves.

As the workshop progresses the trainer introduces the concept of contradiction and begins work with the group on making the decisions outlined in detail in Chapter 7 as a contradiction to the effects of internalized oppression.

In a typical workshop, the men's trainer might ask them to tell one another about:

O   Ways in which they are proud of themselves as men.
O   Their life story as one of triumph over adversity.
O   Times in their lives when they have been able to be their real selves, to be deeply 'connected' to themselves.
O   What happened to cause them to disconnect from themselves.
O   From the perspective of seeing themselves as 'heroic survivors of violence', share times in their lives when they have experienced violence, ridicule or humiliation.
O   What gets in their way of having excellent, close relationships with other men.
O   What they like, admire and appreciate about the other men in the group.

He might also work with the group on the decisions described in more detail in Chapter 9.

These sessions are linked to and develop the theory presentations made to the whole group. The sessions last from one to two hours, and whereas in the early stages participants talk only briefly about themselves, as the safety increases they talk in much more depth. Trainers need the ability to pay excellent attention to people and to be able to listen with complete respect in order to lead such groups, to be relaxed and unconditional in stressful situations, and be able to talk about their own lives with integrity.

WORK IN PAIRS

There are many moments when it is possible to create opportunities for people to work in pairs during the training. These are intended to:

O   Give people a 'space' to talk over how the workshop is going for them and about the personal and leadership issues it raises.
O   Give people the opportunity to practise and improve their ability to pay attention and listen well.
O   Give people the opportunity to learn how to use someone else's attention effectively.

A FORMAT FOR WORK ON ELIMINATING SEXISM

The understanding that people need the opportunity to share with the members of the 'other group' their experience of oppression, how it has hurt them, what they need to do about it, and what help they will need has been crucial in developing a format for successful work on eliminating sexism. I have tried many different approaches in the more than one hundred workshops that I have led. The approach that has worked best comprises a number of stages. They are as follows:

O   The whole group listens to the woman trainer present information about the effects of sexism and internalized oppression on women's lives based upon the information contained in Chapter 6.
O   She then invites other women to share their own experience while the men pay attention and listen with complete respect.
O   When the women have finished, the men withdraw with the male trainer to 'process' what they have heard, to ask any questions they have, and to think about its implications for their relationships with women, their leadership and their support for the equal opportunities policy.

This is often a very difficult session for the men, as they tend to become defensive and to deny what they have heard, to argue that they have heard nothing new, or even to undermine the credibility of the women who have been sharing with them. Great patience and personal strength is needed from all of the trainers to see this through effectively.

Later, the whole group reconvenes, and goes through the next steps:

O   The male trainer presents information about the nature of men's oppression and its effects on men's lives and leadership.
O   He then invites the male participants to share from their own experience.
O   When this is completed, the women withdraw and consider what they have heard and its implications.

CONCLUSION

❖

We are facing a growing crisis of unmanageable competition on a world scale. Attempts to bring some rationality and planning to this situation, such as the GATT Agreement or through the World Bank or the IMF, fall well short of the need for an initiative from world level leadership to ensure that everyone in the world is able to win – that is, to enjoy at least a minimum standard of health care, education and development.

In the absence of such strategies we need to adopt a new system of leadership in our organizations that ensures everyone is able to contribute the best of their thinking and efforts. Pressure from the global marketplace makes it inevitable that the only organizations to survive will be those able to harness the intelligence, creativity and initiative of all their people, and this will only be possible if people feel that they are at the heart of the business.

In a world in which everyone is moving into everyone else's market and the pursuit of excellence tends to push products and services on to a common ground, the only thing to differentiate one organization from another will be the way it can mobilize the energy and abilities of people at all levels, especially those who have been ignored for so long.

However, this is a challenge beset with difficulties. Many organizations in the private and public sectors alike will respond to growing competition by reducing the number of employees year upon year. In particular, this reduction will focus upon layers of management which have historically been safe from what has become known as 'downsizing'. In my work I find that this leaves many people deeply cynical and extremely insecure. The notion that they should commit themselves to an organization which clearly has an instrumental and exploitative relationship with them is greeted with derision by managers and workers alike.

Thus it is important for top management to have a clear aim based upon its vision, purpose and values and then cascading that aim down through the organization in a systematic way. Top management must develop constancy of purpose in pursuing this strategy, and also take the leap of faith that is needed

171

to believe that treating people well will make the difference. Short-term and opportunistic action to cut costs will only cost more in the medium term.

Top management will need to adopt, instead, the long-term path towards an inclusive organization. 'Inclusion' is a new word for an old concept. The desire for 'inclusion' is rapidly becoming the central focus of everyone who feels left out from decision-making and power, whether it is from a neighbourhood group or by central government. People are going to demand that their voice is included, that they are involved and their thinking valued. Organizations will face increasing pressure to work systematically to end the exclusion of any group of people who see themselves as the victims of discrimination and prejudice.

It makes more sense to launch a new leadership initiative aimed at building an inclusive organization. This will liberate energy and commitment throughout the enterprise which will enable it to grow and survive. The challenge is to believe in the people who work in the organization, particularly those people who are generally excluded from contributing their thinking when we are contemplating how to make a decisive improvement in performance. As we develop the ability to believe in people, we will begin to understand what needs to be done to ensure the success of the organization and then we will be able to develop all of the attributes and skills that are essential to involving them effectively.

It is the major theme of the next 25 years. We must work to understand it or we will fail in our endeavours to build viable, self-improving organizations.

SOURCES AND RESOURCES

T his book was conceived as part of a continuing process of developing a deeper understanding of the role of leadership in the modern organization and the special needs of women and men if they are to be able to provide that leadership. So here are some resources to facilitate the transition from my printed pages to your practice.

ORGANIZATIONS

THE B TEAM

320 Commercial Way, London SE15 1QN. Tel: 0171–732 9409.
Produces beautiful photographs of young men in ordinary situations. Particularly useful if you wish to create images of men combining strength with humanity when working with young men.

BRITISH ASSOCIATION OF WOMEN ENTREPRENEURS

8 Eyre Court, London NW8 9TT. Tel: 0171–722 0192.
A network for women who run their own businesses. Provides support and information.

EQUAL OPPORTUNITIES COMMISSION

Overseas House, Quay Street, Manchester M3 3HN. Tel: 0161–833 9244. Government organization responsible for enforcing equal opportunities legislation and providing leadership on research and policy. Produces reports on progress generally and in specific organizations.

NATIONAL ALLIANCE OF WOMEN'S ORGANIZATIONS

279–281 Whitechapel Road, London E1 1BY. Tel: 0171–247 7052.
This is a national umbrella organization for women interested in every aspect of women's advancement.

THE INSTITUTE OF RACE RELATIONS

2–6 Leeke Road, Kings Cross Road, London WC1X 9HX. Tel: 0171–837 0041.
Undertakes research on issues of oppression and social structure and publishes *Race and Class*, a quarterly journal of articles and reviews on social change.

WOMEN IN MANAGEMENT

64 Marryat Road, London SW19 5BN. Tel: 0181–944 6332.
Network for women who are or intend to become managers. This very active women's organization offers development and training and assists women to network across the UK.

WORKING WITH MEN

320 Commercial Way, London SE15 1QN. Tel: 0171–732 9409.
Excellent quarterly journal providing news and debate for men who work with men in whatever way.

RE-EVALUATION COUNSELLING

719 Second Avenue North, Seattle, WA 98109, USA. Tel: 206 284 0031.
International network of people who meet to assist one another to recover their full functioning based upon propositions on the inherent nature of human beings. Provides counselling and client training and opportunities to explore issues of social liberation for all groups.

DEMOS LTD

9 Bridewell Place, London EC4V 6AP. Tel: 0171–353 4479.
Think-tank publishing reports on social behaviour and attitudes in the UK. Produced new report about the current experience and attitudes of young women and men in 1995.

BOOKS AND ARTICLES

KEY BOOKS AND ARTICLES ON ISSUES OF GENDER

Brennan, Rosemary, *Barriers to Women's Leadership* (Industrial and Commercial Training, 1987).
This article was a milestone in the analysis of the internal barriers to women

taking full leadership. It makes proposals for how women and men can work together to overcome them in the work place.

Faludi, Susan, *Backlash* (Chatto and Windus, 1991).
An excellent book laying out the attack on feminism during the 1980s and the route forward in the 1990s.

Jackins, Harvey, *The Human Side of Human Beings* (Rational Island Press, 1971).
A brilliant commentary on the inherent nature of human beings and a cogent explanation of why people behave irrationally.

Marshall, Judi, *Women Managers – Travellers in a Male World* (Wiley, 1984).
Excellent research-based text on the situation facing women in management and the next steps they must take to move forward.

Phillips, Angela, *The Trouble with Boys* (Pandora, 1993).
There has been too little study as yet of what happens to men and its effects on their lives. This is a simple but brilliant explanation of the process of gender conditioning of boys and what needs to happen if we are to bring up our sons with their humanity fully intact.

Spender, Dale, *Man Made Language* (Routledge and Kegan Paul, 1985).
The definitive text on the effect of language upon the value of women.

Woolf, Naomi, *Fire with Fire* (Chatto and Windus, 1993).
Reviews the present situation confronting women and proposes that there is a new female power that will change the twenty-first century.

CLASSIC BOOKS ON LEADERSHIP, SYSTEMS AND EFFECTIVE ORGANIZATIONAL CHANGE

Covey, Stephen, *The Seven Habits of Highly Effective People* (London: Simon & Schuster, 1992).
A powerful and dynamic introduction to the principle–centred leadership so necessary for the next decade.

Deming, E.W., *Out of the Crisis* (Cambridge, MA: MIT Centre for Advanced Engineering Study, 1986).
An introduction to the improvement of productivity and quality by applying the principles and practice of continual improvement.

Deming, E.W., *The New Economics: For Government, Education and Industry* (MIT Press, 1993).
Deming's lask book integrates every aspect of organizational development through his 'System of Profound Knowledge'. A 'must read'.

McGregor, Douglas, *The Human Side of Enterprise* (New York: McGraw-Hill, 1960).
Source of the famous 'Theory X and Theory Y' assumptions of what motivates people and the leadership implications. This remains a 'must' to read and act upon – it still says it all, 35 years later.

Senge, Peter, *The Fifth Discipline* (Century Business, 1990).
A new introduction to the application of systems theory to improving organizational performance by creating an organization that can understand itself as a system and engage in ongoing learning.

Jacobs, Robert W., *Real Time Strategic Change* (San Francisco: Berrett-Koehler, 1994).
Introduces the concept of creating organizational alignment through large group meetings that enable any number of people to plan their collective future.

CONSULTING AND TRAINING ORGANIZATIONS

Listed here are people and organizations which I can personally recommend because I know them well and have experience of their work.

ROSIE BRENNAN

19 Alpha Road, Bristol BS3 1DH. Tel: 01179–879032.
Provides excellent leadership development and training on a wide range of equality issues, particularly for women.

CADWELL CONSULTING AND TRAINING

96 Trees Road, Mount Merion, Dublin, County Dublin. Tel: 003531–2845008.
This Irish company provides consulting and training on the implementation of equality strategies and leadership development for women and men.

THE NETWORK FOR A NEW MEN'S LEADERSHIP

45 Nutgrove Avenue, Bristol BS3 4QF. Tel: 01179–407254.
This is the only UK national leadership development organization for men. It was founded in 1986 and has trained more than 500 men in the principles and practice of non-sexist leadership.

TREFOR LLOYD

320 Commercial Way, London SE15 1QN. Tel: 0171–732 9409.
Provides specialist training for people who work with young men in care, education and youth club situations.

SIMMONS CONSULTING AND TRAINING (SCT)

45 Nutgrove Avenue, Bristol BS3 4QF. Tel: 01179–407254.
Provides consultation to top management on strategy for building an inclusive organization, leadership development in the context of equality for middle managers and awareness training on all aspects of equality for people throughout the enterprise.

INDEX